Exam AZ-104:

Microsoft Azure Administrator

<u>Exclusive Preparation</u>

Achieve success in your AZ-104 Exam on the first try with our new and exclusive preparation book.

This comprehensive resource is designed to help you test your knowledge, providing a collection of the latest questions with detailed explanations and references.

Save both time and money by investing in this book, which covers all the topics included in the AZ-104 exam.

Dedicate your effort to mastering these AZ-104 exam questions, as they offer up-to-date information on the entire exam syllabus.

This book is strategically crafted to not only assess your knowledge and skills but also to boost your confidence for the real exam.

With a focus on thorough preparation, passing the actual AZ-104 Exam on your initial attempt becomes achievable through diligent study of these valuable resources.

The AZ-104 exam consists of approximately 40 to 60 questions, and candidates are allotted 120 minutes to complete the test. To pass the exam, a minimum score of 700 is required, and there is no penalty for incorrect answers.

Examination Focus Areas:

1) Azure Identities and Governance Management (20–25%)

Proficiency in managing Azure identities and implementing governance measures is evaluated in this section.

2) Storage Implementation and Management (15–20%)

This portion assesses the candidate's ability to deploy and manage storage solutions within the Azure environment.

3) Azure Compute Resources Deployment and Management (20–25%)

Candidates are tested on their skills in deploying and managing compute resources in the Azure platform.

4) Virtual Networking Implementation and Management (15–20%)

This category evaluates the candidate's competence in implementing and managing virtual networking components within Azure.

5) Azure Resource Monitoring and Maintenance (10–15%)

This section gauges the candidate's capability to monitor and sustain Azure resources effectively.

These skill measurement areas outline the key competencies tested in the exam, emphasizing the importance of expertise in managing Azure identities, storage, compute resources, virtual networking, and resource monitoring for successful examination performance.

Practice Test I

1) Your organization comprises multiple departments, each with several virtual machines (VMs) located in the Azure subscription's resource group named RG1. To associate each VM with its respective department, what action should you take?

A. Establish Azure Management Groups for each department.

B. Create a resource group for each department.

C. Assign tags to the virtual machines.

D. Modify the settings of the virtual machines.

2) Your company utilizes an Azure Active Directory (Azure AD) subscription, and you aim to implement an Azure AD conditional access policy. The policy should mandate members of the Global Administrators group to use Multi-Factor Authentication

and an Azure AD-joined device when accessing Azure AD from untrusted locations. In the proposed solution, you access the multi-factor authentication page to modify user settings.

Does this solution meet the goal?

A. Yes

B. No

3) In the context of implementing an Azure AD conditional access policy requiring Global Administrators to use Multi-Factor Authentication and an Azure AD-joined device from untrusted locations, the solution involves accessing the Azure portal to modify the session control of the Azure AD conditional access policy.

Does this solution meet the goal?

A. Yes

B. No

4) For the implementation of an Azure AD conditional access policy demanding Global Administrators to use Multi-Factor Authentication and an Azure AD-joined device from untrusted locations, the solution involves accessing the Azure portal to alter the grant control of the Azure AD conditional access policy.

Does this solution meet the goal?

A. Yes

B. No

5) When planning to deploy an Ubuntu Server virtual machine to your company's Azure subscription, including the addition of a specific trusted root certification authority (CA), which of the following should you use to create the virtual machine?

A. The New-AzureRmVm cmdlet.

B. The New-AzVM cmdlet.

C. The Create-AzVM cmdlet.

D. The az vm create command.

6) Your company employs Multi-Factor Authentication with the Per Authentication option configured. After acquiring a smaller business, it's necessary to enable Multi-Factor Authentication for the new employees, requiring the Per Enabled User setting. The proposed solution involves reconfiguring the existing usage model via the Azure portal.

Does this solution meet the goal?

A. Yes

B. No

7) In a scenario where your company's Azure solution utilizes Multi-Factor

Authentication with the Per Authentication option configured, and new employees from an acquired business need Multi-Factor Authentication with the Per Enabled User setting, the proposed solution involves reconfiguring the existing usage model via the Azure CLI.

Does this solution meet the goal?

A. Yes

B. No

8) In a situation where Multi-Factor Authentication is in use with the Per Authentication option, and new employees need the Per Enabled User setting after a business acquisition, the proposed solution involves creating a new Multi-Factor Authentication provider with data backup from the existing provider.

Does this solution meet the goal?

A. Yes

B. No

9) In the context of an Azure AD tenant configured for hybrid coexistence with on-premises Active Directory, a new user account is created in the on-premise Active Directory. To replicate the user information to Azure AD immediately, the proposed solution involves running the Start-ADSyncSyncCycle -PolicyType Initial PowerShell cmdlet.

Does this solution meet the goal?

A. Yes

B. No

10) With an Azure AD tenant configured for hybrid coexistence with on-premises Active Directory and a DirSync server named DirSync1, the goal is to replicate a new user account's information to Azure

AD immediately. The proposed solution involves using Active Directory Sites and Services to force replication of the Global Catalog on a domain controller.

Does this solution meet the goal?

A. Yes

B. No

11) Your company has an Azure Active Directory (Azure AD) tenant named weyland.com that is configured for hybrid coexistence with the on-premises Active Directory domain. You have a server named DirSync1 that is configured as a DirSync server. You create a new user account in the on-premise Active Directory.

You now need to replicate the user information to Azure AD immediately.

Solution: You restart the NetLogon service on a domain controller.

Does the solution meet the goal?

A. Yes

B. No

12) Your company has a Microsoft Azure subscription. The company has datacenters in Los Angeles and New York. You are configuring the two datacenters as geo-clustered sites for site resiliency. You need to recommend an Azure storage redundancy option. You have the following data storage requirements:

Data must be stored on multiple nodes.

Data must be stored on nodes in separate geographic locations.

Data can be read from the secondary location as well as from the primary location.

Which of the following Azure stored redundancy options should you recommend?

A. Geo-redundant storage

B. Read-only geo-redundant storage

C. Zone-redundant storage

D. Locally redundant storage

13) Your company has an Azure subscription that includes a storage account, a resource group, a blob container, and a file share. A colleague named Jon Ross makes use of a solitary Azure Resource Manager (ARM) template to deploy a virtual machine and an additional Azure Storage account. You want to review the ARM template that was used by Jon Ross.

Solution: You access the Virtual Machine blade.

Does the solution meet the goal?

A. Yes

B. No

14) Your company has an Azure subscription that includes a storage account, a resource group, a blob container, and a file share. A colleague named Jon Ross makes use of a solitary Azure Resource Manager (ARM) template to deploy a virtual machine and an additional Azure Storage account. You want to review the ARM template that was used by Jon Ross.

Solution: You access the Resource Group blade.

Does the solution meet the goal?

A. Yes

B. No

15) Your company has an Azure subscription that includes a storage account, a resource group, a blob

container, and a file share. A colleague named Jon Ross makes use of a solitary Azure Resource Manager (ARM) template to deploy a virtual machine and an additional Azure Storage account. You want to review the ARM template that was used by Jon Ross.

Solution: You access the Container blade.

Does the solution meet the goal?

A. Yes

B. No

16) Your company has three virtual machines (VMs) that are included in an availability set. You try to resize one of the VMs, which returns an allocation failure message. It is imperative that the VM is resized.

Which of the following actions should you take?

A. You should only stop one of the VMs.

B. You should stop two of the VMs.

C. You should stop all three VMs.

D. You should remove the necessary VM from the availability set.

17) You have an Azure virtual machine (VM) that has a single data disk. You have been tasked with attaching this data disk to another Azure VM. You need to make sure that your strategy allows for the virtual machines to be offline for the least amount of time possible.

Which of the following is the action you should take FIRST?

A. Stop the VM that includes the data disk.

B. Stop the VM that the data disk must be attached to.

C. Detach the data disk.

D. Delete the VM that includes the data disk.

18) Your company has an Azure subscription. You need to deploy a number of Azure virtual machines (VMs) using Azure Resource Manager (ARM) templates. You have been informed that the VMs will be included in a single availability set. You are required to make sure that the ARM template you configure allows for as many VMs as possible to remain accessible in the event of fabric failure or maintenance.

Which of the following is the value that you should configure for the platformFaultDomainCount property?

A. 10

B. 30

C. Min Value

D. Max Value

19) Your company has an Azure subscription. You need to deploy a number of Azure virtual machines (VMs) using Azure Resource Manager (ARM) templates. You have been informed that the VMs will be included in a single availability set. You are required to make sure that the ARM template you configure allows for as many VMs as possible to remain accessible in the event of fabric failure or maintenance.

Which of the following is the value that you should configure for the platformUpdateDomainCount property?

A. 10

B. 20

C. 30

D. 40

20) DRAG DROP -

You have downloaded an Azure Resource Manager (ARM) template to deploy numerous virtual machines (VMs).

The ARM template is based on a current VM but must be adapted to reference an administrative password.

You need to make sure that the password cannot be stored in plain text.

You are preparing to create the necessary components to achieve your goal.

Which of the following should you create to achieve your goal? Answer by choosing the correct option from the list to the answer area.

Select and Place:

Options:

a) An Azure Key Vault

b) An Azure Storage Account

c) Azure Active Directory (AD) Identity Protection

d) An Access Policy

e) An Azure Policy

f) A Backup Policy

Answer:

1)...

2)...

21) In the context of your Azure AD hybrid environment with on-premises VMs, you want to automate the configuration of new VMs using PowerShell scripts. Which solution is most suitable for ensuring these scripts run on the new VMs?

A. Utilize a SetupComplete.cmd batch file in the %windir%\setup\scripts directory.

B. Implement a Group Policy Object (GPO) to execute the scripts as logon scripts.

C. Implement a Group Policy Object (GPO) to execute the scripts as startup scripts.

D. Place the scripts in a new virtual hard disk (VHD).

22) In your Azure AD hybrid environment, you plan to deploy new VMs in Azure with identical operating systems and custom software requirements. You have created a reference VM in the on-premise virtual environment, generalized it, and now want to upload the image to Azure for future deployments. Which PowerShell cmdlet(s) should you use?

A. Add-AzVM

B. Add-AzVhd

C. Add-AzImage

D. Add-AzImageDataDisk

23) DRAG DROP -

Your company has an Azure subscription that includes a number of Azure virtual

machines (VMs), which are all part of the same virtual network.

Your company also has an on-premises Hyper-V server that hosts a VM, named VM1, which must be replicated to Azure.

Which of the following objects that must be created to achieve this goal?

Select and Place:

Options:

a) Hyper-V Site

b) Storage Account

c) Azure Recovery Services Vault

d) Azure Traffic Manager Instance

e) Replication Policy

f) Endpoint

Answers:

1)...

2)...

3)...

24) Your company's Azure subscription includes two Azure networks named VirtualNetworkA and VirtualNetworkB.

VirtualNetworkA includes a VPN gateway that is configured to make use of static routing. Also, a site-to-site VPN connection exists between your company's on-premises network and VirtualNetworkA.

You have configured a point-to-site VPN connection to VirtualNetworkA from a workstation running Windows 10. After configuring virtual network peering between VirtualNetworkA and VirtualNetworkB, you confirm that you are able to access VirtualNetworkB from the company's on-premises network. However, you find that you cannot establish a connection to VirtualNetworkB from the Windows 10 workstation.

You have to make sure that a connection to VirtualNetworkB can be established from the Windows 10 workstation.

Solution: You choose the Allow gateway transit setting on VirtualNetworkA.

Does the solution meet the goal?

A. Yes

B. No

25) Your company's Azure subscription includes two Azure networks named VirtualNetworkA and VirtualNetworkB.

VirtualNetworkA includes a VPN gateway that is configured to make use of static routing. Also, a site-to-site VPN connection exists between your company's on-premises network and VirtualNetworkA.

You have configured a point-to-site VPN connection to VirtualNetworkA from a workstation running Windows 10. After configuring virtual network peering between VirtualNetworkA and VirtualNetworkB, you confirm that you are able to access VirtualNetworkB from the company's on-premises network.

However, you find that you cannot establish a connection to VirtualNetworkB from the Windows 10 workstation.

You have to make sure that a connection to VirtualNetworkB can be established from the Windows 10 workstation.

Solution: You choose the Allow gateway transit setting on VirtualNetworkB.

Does the solution meet the goal?

A. Yes

B. No

26) Your company's Azure subscription includes two Azure networks named VirtualNetworkA and VirtualNetworkB.

VirtualNetworkA includes a VPN gateway that is configured to make use of static routing. Also, a site-to-site VPN connection exists between your company's on-premises network and VirtualNetworkA.

You have configured a point-to-site VPN connection to VirtualNetworkA from a workstation running Windows 10. After configuring virtual network peering between VirtualNetworkA and VirtualNetworkB, you confirm that you are able to access VirtualNetworkB from the company's on-premises network. However, you find that you cannot establish a connection to VirtualNetworkB from the Windows 10 workstation.

You have to make sure that a connection to VirtualNetworkB can be established from the Windows 10 workstation.

Solution: You download and re-install the VPN client configuration package on the Windows 10 workstation.

Does the solution meet the goal?

A. Yes

B. No

27) Your company has virtual machines (VMs) hosted in Microsoft Azure. The VMs are located in a single Azure virtual network named VNet1.

The company has users that work remotely. The remote workers require access to the VMs on VNet1.

You need to provide access for the remote workers.

What should you do?

A. Configure a Site-to-Site (S2S) VPN.

B. Configure a VNet-toVNet VPN.

C. Configure a Point-to-Site (P2S) VPN.

D. Configure DirectAccess on a Windows Server 2012 server VM.

E. Configure a Multi-Site VPN

28) Your company has a Microsoft SQL Server Always On availability group configured on their Azure virtual machines (VMs).

You need to configure an Azure internal load balancer as a listener for the availability group.

Solution: You create an HTTP health probe on port 1433.

Does the solution meet the goal?

A. Yes

B. No

29) Your company has a Microsoft SQL Server Always On availability group configured on their Azure virtual machines (VMs).

You need to configure an Azure internal load balancer as a listener for the availability group.

Solution: You set Session persistence to Client IP.

27

Does the solution meet the goal?

A. Yes

B. No

30) Your company has a Microsoft SQL Server Always On availability group configured on their Azure virtual machines (VMs).

You need to configure an Azure internal load balancer as a listener for the availability group.

Solution: You enable Floating IP.

Does the solution meet the goal?

A. Yes

B. No

31) Your company has two on-premises servers named SRV01 and SRV02.

Developers have created an application that runs on SRV01. The application calls a service on SRV02 by IP address.

You plan to migrate the application to Azure virtual machines (VMs). You have configured two VMs on a single subnet in an Azure virtual network.

You need to configure the two VMs with static internal IP addresses.

What should you do?

A. Run the New-AzureRMVMConfig PowerShell cmdlet.

B. Run the Set-AzureSubnet PowerShell cmdlet.

C. Modify the VM properties in the Azure Management Portal.

D. Modify the IP properties in Windows Network and Sharing Center.

E. Run the Set-AzureStaticVNetIP PowerShell cmdlet.

32) Your company has an Azure Active Directory (Azure AD) subscription.

You need to deploy five virtual machines (VMs) to your company's virtual network subnet.

The VMs will each have both a public and private IP address. Inbound and outbound security rules for all of these virtual machines must be identical.

Which of the following is the least amount of network interfaces needed for this configuration?

A. 5

B. 10

C. 20

D. 40

33) Your company has an Azure Active Directory (Azure AD) subscription.

You need to deploy five virtual machines (VMs) to your company's virtual network subnet.

The VMs will each have both a public and private IP address. Inbound and outbound security rules for all of these virtual machines must be identical.

Which of the following is the least amount of security groups needed for this configuration?

A. 4

B. 3

C. 2

D. 1

34) Your company's Azure subscription includes Azure virtual machines (VMs) that run Windows Server 2016.

One of the VMs is backed up every day using Azure Backup Instant Restore.

When the VM becomes infected with data encrypting ransomware, you decide to recover the VM's files.

Which of the following is TRUE in this scenario?

A. You can only recover the files to the infected VM.

B. You can recover the files to any VM within the company's subscription.

C. You can only recover the files to a new VM.

D. You will not be able to recover the files.

35) Your company's Azure subscription includes Azure virtual machines (VMs) that run Windows Server 2016.

One of the VMs is backed up every day using Azure Backup Instant Restore.

When the VM becomes infected with data encrypting ransomware, you are required to restore the VM.

Which of the following actions should you take?

A. You should restore the VM after deleting the infected VM.

B. You should restore the VM to any VM within the company's subscription.

C. You should restore the VM to a new Azure VM.

D. You should restore the VM to an on-premise Windows device.

36) You administer a solution in Azure that is currently having performance issues.

You need to find the cause of the performance issues pertaining to metrics on the Azure infrastructure.

Which of the following is the tool you should use?

A. Azure Traffic Analytics

B. Azure Monitor

C. Azure Activity Log

D. Azure Advisor

37) Your company has an Azure subscription that includes a Recovery Services vault.

You want to use Azure Backup to schedule a backup of your company's virtual machines (VMs) to the Recovery Services vault.

Which of the following VMs can you back up? Choose all that apply.

A. VMs that run Windows 10.

B. VMs that run Windows Server 2012 or higher.

C. VMs that have NOT been shut down.

D. VMs that run Debian 8.2+.

E. VMs that have been shut down.

38) You have an Azure Active Directory (Azure AD) tenant named contoso.com.

You have a CSV file that contains the names and email addresses of 500 external users.

You need to create a guest user account in contoso.com for each of the 500 external users.

Solution: You create a PowerShell script that runs the New-AzureADUser cmdlet for each user.

Does this meet the goal?

A. Yes

B. No

39) You have an Azure Active Directory (Azure AD) tenant named contoso.com.

You have a CSV file that contains the names and email addresses of 500 external users.

You need to create a guest user account in contoso.com for each of the 500 external users.

Solution: From Azure AD in the Azure portal, you use the Bulk create user operation.

Does this meet the goal?

A. Yes

B. No

40) You have an Azure Active Directory (Azure AD) tenant named contoso.com.

You have a CSV file that contains the names and email addresses of 500 external users.

You need to create a guest user account in contoso.com for each of the 500 external users.

Solution: You create a PowerShell script that runs the New-AzureADMSInvitation cmdlet for each external user.

Does this meet the goal?

A. Yes

B. No

41) HOTSPOT -

You have an Azure subscription named Subscription1 that contains a resource group named RG1.

In RG1, you create an internal load balancer named LB1 and a public load balancer named LB2.

You need to ensure that an administrator named Admin1 can manage LB1 and LB2. The solution must follow the principle of least privilege.

Which role should you assign to Admin1 for each task?

To answer, choose the appropriate options in the answer area.

Hot Area:

Answer area:

1) To add a backend pool to LB1:

   a) Contributor on LB1

   b) Network contributor on RG1

   c) Owner on LB1

2) To add a health probe to LB2:

   a) Contributor on LB2

   b) Network contributor on RG1

   c) Owner on LB2

42) You have an Azure subscription that contains an Azure Active Directory (Azure AD) tenant named contoso.com and an Azure Kubernetes Service (AKS) cluster named AKS1.

An administrator reports that she is unable to grant access to AKS1 to the users in contoso.com.

You need to ensure that access to AKS1 can be granted to the contoso.com users.

What should you do first?

A. From contoso.com, modify the Organization relationships settings.

B. From contoso.com, create an OAuth 2.0 authorization endpoint.

C. Recreate AKS1.

D. From AKS1, create a namespace.

43) You have a Microsoft 365 tenant and an Azure Active Directory (Azure AD) tenant named contoso.com.

You plan to grant three users named User1, User2, and User3 access to a temporary Microsoft SharePoint document library named Library1.

You need to create groups for the users. The solution must ensure that the groups are deleted automatically after 180 days.

Which two groups should you create?

Each correct answer presents a complete solution.

A. a Microsoft 365 group that uses the Assigned membership type

B. a Security group that uses the Assigned membership type

C. a Microsoft 365 group that uses the Dynamic User membership type

D. a Security group that uses the Dynamic User membership type

E. a Security group that uses the Dynamic Device membership type

44) HOTSPOT –

You have an Azure Active Directory (Azure

AD) tenant named contoso.com that contains the users shown in the following table:

Name	Type	Member of
User1	Member	Group1
User2	Guest	Group1
User3	Member	None
UserA	Member	Group2
UserB	Guest	Group2

User3 is the owner of Group1. Group2 is a member of Group1. You configure an access review named Review1 as shown in the following exhibit:

Create an access review ▫ ⊠

Access reviews enable reviewers to attest user's membership in a group or access to an application.

* Review name	Review1
Description ❶	
* Start date	2018-11-22 📅
Frequency	One time ⌄
Duration (in days) ⊘ ◯	1
End ❶	(Never End by Occurrence)
* Number of times	0
* End date	2018-12-22 📅

Users

Users to review	Members of a group ⌄
Scope	⦿ Guest users only
	◯ Everyone

* Group
Group1   >

Reviewers

Reviewers	Group owners ⌄

Programs

Link to program
Default program   >

⌄ Upon completion settings

⌄ Adavnced settings

For each of the following statements, choose Yes if the statement is true. Otherwise, select No.

Hot Area:

Answer area:

Statements:

1) User3 can perform an access review of User1

2) User3 can perform an access review of UserA

3) User3 can perform an access review of UserB

45) HOTSPOT –

You have the Azure management groups shown in the following table:

Name	In management group
Tenant Root Group	*Not applicable*
ManagementGroup11	Tenant Root Group
ManagementGroup12	Tenant Root Group
ManagementGroup21	ManagementGroup11

You add Azure subscriptions to the management groups as shown in the following table:

Name	Management group
Subscription1	ManagementGroup21
Subscription2	ManagementGroup12

You create the Azure policies shown in the following table:

Name	Parameter	Scope
Not allowed resource types	virtualNetworks	Tenant Root Group
Allowed resource types	virtualNetworks	ManagementGroup12

For each of the following statements,

choose Yes if the statement is true. Otherwise, select No.

Hot Area:

Answer area:

Statements:

1) You can create a Virtual Network in Subscription1

2) You can create a Virtual Machine in Subscription2

3) You can add Subscription1 to ManagementGroup11

46) You have an Azure policy as shown in the following exhibit:

SCOPE

* Scope (Learn more about setting the scope)

Subscription 1

Exclusions

Subscription 1/ContosoRG1

BASICS

* Policy definition

Not allowed resource types

* Assignment name ❶

Not allowed resource types

Assignment ID

/subscriptions/5eb8d0b6-ce3b-4ce0-a631-9f5321bedabb/providers/Microsoft.Authorization/policyAssignments/0e6fb866bf854f54accae2a9

Description

Assigned by

admin1@contoso.com

PARAMETERS

* Not allowed resource types ❶

Microsoft.Sql/servers

What is the effect of the policy?

A. You are prevented from creating Azure SQL servers anywhere in Subscription 1.

B. You can create Azure SQL servers in ContosoRG1 only.

C. You are prevented from creating Azure SQL Servers in ContosoRG1 only.

D. You can create Azure SQL servers in any resource group within Subscription 1.

47) HOTSPOT –

You have an Azure subscription that contains the resources shown in the following table:

Name	Type	Resource group	Tag
RG6	Resource group	*Not applicable*	*None*
VNET1	Virtual network	RG6	Department: D1

You assign a policy to RG6 as shown in the following table:

Section	Setting	Value
Scope	Scope	Subscription1/RG6
	Exclusions	*None*
Basics	Policy definition	Apply tag and its default value
	Assignment name	Apply tag and its default value
Parameters	Tag name	Label
	Tag value	Value1

To RG6, you apply the tag: RGroup: RG6. You deploy a virtual network named VNET2 to RG6.

Which tags apply to VNET1 and VNET2?

Hot Area:

Answer area:

1) VNET1:

a) None

b) Department: D1 only

c) Department: D1, and RGroup: RG6 only

d) Department: D1, and Label: Value1 only

e) Department: D1, RGroup: RG6, and Label: Value1

2) VNET2

   a) None

   b) RGroup: RG6 only

   c) Label: Value1 only

   d) RGroup: RG6, and Label: Value1

48) You have an Azure subscription named AZPT1 that contains the resources shown in the following table:

Name	Type
storage1	Azure Storage account
VNET1	Virtual network
VM1	Azure virtual machine
VM1Managed	Managed disk for VM1
RVAULT1	Recovery Services vault for the site recovery of VM1

You create a new Azure subscription named AZPT2.
You need to identify which resources can be moved to AZPT2.

Which resources should you identify?

A. VM1, storage1, VNET1, and VM1Managed only

B. VM1 and VM1Managed only

C. VM1, storage1, VNET1, VM1Managed, and RVAULT1

D. RVAULT1 only

49) You recently created a new Azure subscription that contains a user named Admin1.

Admin1 attempts to deploy an Azure Marketplace resource by using an Azure Resource Manager template. Admin1 deploys the template by using Azure

PowerShell and receives the following error message: `User failed validation to purchase resources. Error message: `Legal terms have not been accepted for this item on this subscription. To accept legal terms, please go to the Azure portal (http://go.microsoft.com/fwlink/?LinkId=5 34873) and configure programmatic deployment for the Marketplace item or create it there for the first time. `

You need to ensure that Admin1 can deploy the Marketplace resource successfully.

What should you do?

A. From Azure PowerShell, run the Set-AzApiManagementSubscription cmdlet

B. From the Azure portal, register the Microsoft.Marketplace resource provider

C. From Azure PowerShell, run the Set-AzMarketplaceTerms cmdlet

D. From the Azure portal, assign the Billing administrator role to Admin1

50) You have an Azure Active Directory (Azure AD) tenant that contains 5,000 user accounts.

You create a new user account named AdminUser1.

You need to assign the User administrator administrative role to AdminUser1.

What should you do from the user account properties?

A. From the Licenses blade, assign a new license

B. From the Directory role blade, modify the directory role

C. From the Groups blade, invite the user account to a new group

51) You have an Azure Active Directory (Azure AD) tenant with 100 user accounts named contoso.onmicrosoft.com. You

purchase 10 Azure AD Premium P2 licenses for the tenant.

What action should you take to ensure that 10 users can utilize all the Azure AD Premium features?

A. Assign a license from the Licenses blade of Azure AD.

B. Invite the users to a group from the Groups blade of each user.

C. Add an enterprise application from the Azure AD domain.

D. Modify the directory role from the Directory role blade of each user.

52) You have an Azure subscription named Subscription1 and an on-premises deployment of Microsoft System Center Service Manager. Within Subscription1, there is a virtual machine named VM1.

What is the initial step you should take to ensure that an alert is triggered in Service

Manager when the available memory on VM1 falls below 10 percent?

A. Create an automation runbook.

B. Deploy a function app.

C. Deploy the IT Service Management Connector (ITSM).

D. Create a notification.

53) You have signed up for Azure Active Directory (Azure AD) Premium P2. You need to grant administrative privileges to a user named admin1@contoso.com on all the computers that will be joined to the Azure AD domain.

What configuration should you perform in Azure AD?

A. Configure device settings from the Devices blade.

B. Configure providers from the MFA Server blade.

C. Configure user settings from the Users blade.

D. Configure general settings from the Groups blade.

54) HOTSPOT –

You have Azure Active Directory tenant named Contoso.com that includes following users:

Name	Role
User1	Cloud device administrator
User2	User administrator

Contoso.com includes following Windows 10 devices:

Name	Join type
Device1	Azure AD registered
Device2	Azure AD joined

You create following security groups in Contoso.com:

Name	Membership Type	Owner
Group1	Assigned	User2
Group2	Dynamic Device	User2

For each of the following statements, select Yes if the statement is true. Otherwise, select No.

Hot Area:

Answer area:

Statements:

1) User1 can add Device2 to Group1

2) User2 can add Device1 to Group1

3) User2 can add Device2 to Group2

55) You have an Azure subscription that contains a resource group named RG26. RG26 is set to the West Europe location and is used to create temporary resources for a project. RG26 contains the resources shown in the following table.

Name	Type	Location
VM1	Virtual machine	North Europe
RGV1	Recovery Services vault	North Europe
SQLD01	SQL server in Azure VM	North Europe
sa001	Storage account	West Europe

SQLDB01 is backed up to RGV1. When the project is complete, you attempt to delete RG26 from the Azure portal. The deletion fails.

You need to delete RG26. What should you do first?

A. Delete VM1

B. Stop VM1

C. Stop the backup of SQLDB01

D. Delete sa001

56) You have an Azure subscription named Subscription1 that contains a virtual

network named VNet1. VNet1 is in a resource group named RG1.

Subscription1 has a user named User1 with the roles Reader, Security Admin, and Security Reader. You need to ensure that User1 can assign the Reader role for VNet1 to other users.

What should you do?

A. Remove User1 from the Security Reader and Reader roles for Subscription1.

B. Assign User1 the User Access Administrator role for VNet1.

C. Assign User1 the Network Contributor role for VNet1.

D. Assign User1 the Network Contributor role for RG1.

57) You have an Azure Active Directory (Azure AD) tenant named contosocloud.onmicrosoft.com.

Your company has a public DNS zone for contoso.com.

You add contoso.com as a custom domain name to Azure AD.

You need to ensure that Azure can verify the domain name.

Which type of DNS record should you create?

A. MX

B. NSEC

C. PTR

D. RRSIG

58) You have an Azure Directory (Azure AD) tenant named Adatum and an Azure Subscription named Subscription1.

Adatum contains a group named Developers. Subscription1 contains a resource group named Dev.

You need to provide the Developers group with the ability to create Azure logic apps in the Dev resource group.

Solution: On Subscription1, you assign the DevTest Labs User role to the Developers group. Does this meet the goal?

A. Yes

B. No

59) You have an Azure Directory (Azure AD) tenant named Adatum and an Azure Subscription named Subscription1.

Adatum contains a group named Developers. Subscription1 contains a resource group named Dev.

You need to provide the Developers group with the ability to create Azure logic apps in the Dev resource group.

Solution: On Subscription1, you assign the Logic App Operator role to the Developers group. Does this meet the goal?

A. Yes

B. No

60) You have an Azure Directory (Azure AD) tenant named Adatum and an Azure Subscription named Subscription1.

Adatum contains a group named Developers. Subscription1 contains a resource group named Dev.

You need to provide the Developers group with the ability to create Azure logic apps in the Dev resource group.

Solution: On Dev, you assign the Contributor role to the Developers group. Does this meet the goal?

A. Yes

B. No

Answers and Explanation

1) Correct answer: C

While creating separate resource groups for each department is a common approach to logically organize resources, using tags can also be a valid method for associating virtual machines with their respective departments. Tags are metadata that can be applied to Azure resources, providing a flexible way to categorize and organize resources.

So, the corrected answer is:

C. Assign tags to the virtual machines.

Reference:

https://docs.microsoft.com/en-us/azure/azure-resource-manager/resource-group-using-tags

2) Correct answer: B

1- the best way to enforce MFA is by Conditional Access.

2- the device has to be identified by azure AD as AAD joined Device.

3- the trusted IP must be configured.

The proposed solution does not meet the goal. The reason is that modifying user settings on the multi-factor authentication page does not enforce conditional access policies. Conditional access policies are configured separately and are used to control access to applications and resources based on specific conditions, such as user group membership, device compliance, or location.

To achieve the goal of mandating members of the Global Administrators group to use Multi-Factor Authentication and an Azure AD-joined device when accessing Azure AD from untrusted locations, you should configure an Azure AD conditional access policy. This policy can be set up in the Azure portal, specifying the required conditions, including the use of Multi-Factor Authentication and the device type.

In summary, the correct approach is to configure a conditional access policy rather than modifying user settings on the multi-factor authentication page.

3) Correct answer: B

The solution described, involving modifying the session control of the Azure AD conditional access policy through the Azure portal, does not meet the goal. The session control typically refers to settings related to user sessions, such as single sign-on and session management. To enforce Multi-Factor Authentication and device requirements for Global Administrators from untrusted locations, you need to configure specific conditions within the conditional access policy itself, not just the session control settings.

To achieve the goal of requiring Global Administrators to use Multi-Factor Authentication and an Azure AD-joined device when accessing Azure AD from untrusted locations, you should set up the appropriate conditions directly within the conditional access policy in the Azure portal.

You alter the grant control, not session control.

4) Correct answer: A

There is another copy of this question that mentions going to the MFA page in Azure Portal as the solution = incorrect. On that page you can't make a Conditional Access Policy.

I did this in lab step by step:

- The Answer "A" is correct

- Instead of the MFA page mentioned above, you have to go the route of Conditional Access Policy-->Grant Control mentioned here for this question. Under Grant Control you are given the option of setting MFA and requiring AD joined devices in the exact same window.

Reference:

https://docs.microsoft.com/en-us/azure/active-directory/conditional-access/concept-conditional-access-grant

5) Correct answer: D

If you are using the Azure Command-Line Interface (CLI), the correct option for deploying an Ubuntu Server virtual machine, including the addition of a specific trusted root certification authority (CA), is indeed:

D. The az vm create command.

The az vm create command in the Azure CLI allows you to create a new virtual machine, and it provides options to specify various settings, including the configuration of trusted root certificates. Therefore, if you are using the Azure CLI, option D is the appropriate choice for the given scenario.

It specifically mentions clout-init.txt. on the following link:

https://docs.microsoft.com/en-us/azure/virtual-machines/linux/using-cloud-init

The az vm create command. you need to create an Ubuntu Linux VM using a cloud-init script for configuration.

For example, az vm create -g MyResourceGroup -n MyVm --image debian --custom-data MyCloudInitScript.yml

Reference:

https://docs.microsoft.com/en-us/cli/azure/vm?view=azure-cli-latest

https://cloudinit.readthedocs.io/en/latest/topics/examples.html

6) Correct answer: B

The proposed solution does not meet the goal. To enable Multi-Factor Authentication for new employees with the Per Enabled User setting, you typically need to configure this setting directly in the Multi-Factor Authentication settings, not within the usage model.

To achieve the goal, you should access the Multi-Factor Authentication settings in the Azure portal and specifically enable the Per Enabled User setting for the new employees. Adjusting the usage model alone may not address the requirement to enable Multi-Factor Authentication on a per-user basis.

Since it is not possible to change the usage model of an existing provider as it is right now, you have to create a new one and reactivate your existing server with activation credentials from the new provider.

Reference:

https://365lab.net/2015/04/11/switch-usage-model-in-azure-multi-factor-authentication-server/

7) Correct answer: B

The proposed solution involving reconfiguring the existing usage model via the Azure CLI does not meet the goal. The "Per Enabled User" setting for Multi-Factor Authentication is typically configured at the user level, not through the usage model.

To meet the goal of enabling Multi-Factor Authentication for new employees with the "Per Enabled User" setting, you should adjust the settings for each user individually or use user-based policies. Modifying the usage model alone may not address the requirement to enable Multi-Factor Authentication on a per-user basis.

You cannot change the usage model after creating the provider.

Since it is not possible to change the usage model of an existing provider as it is right now, you have to create a new one and reactivate your existing server with activation credentials from the new provider.

Reference:

https://365lab.net/2015/04/11/switch-usage-model-in-azure-multi-factor-authentication-server/

8) Correct answer: B

If the goal is to enable the "Per Enabled User" setting for new employees after a business acquisition, creating a new Multi-Factor Authentication provider with data backup from the existing provider might not be the most direct or appropriate solution.

In typical scenarios, adjusting the Multi-Factor Authentication settings at the provider level may not achieve the goal of enabling the "Per Enabled User" setting for specific users. The "Per Enabled User" setting is usually applied at the user level, and configuring it often involves modifying individual user settings or using user-specific policies.

Therefore, the corrected response is:

B. No

Effective September 1st, 2018 new auth providers may no longer be created. Existing auth providers may continue to be used and updated, but migration is no longer possible. Multi-factor authentication will continue to be available as a feature in Azure AD Premium licenses.

Reference:

https://docs.microsoft.com/en-us/azure/active-directory/authentication/concept-mfa-authprovider

9) Correct answer: B

Initial will perform a full sync and add the user account created but it will take time, Delta, will kick off a delta sync and bring only the last change, so it will be "immediately" and will fulfill the requirements.

The proposed solution, involving running the Start-ADSyncSyncCycle -PolicyType Initial PowerShell cmdlet, does not meet the goal of replicating user information to Azure AD immediately.

In an Azure AD tenant configured for hybrid coexistence with on-premises Active Directory, to initiate an immediate synchronization of a new user account, you should use the following PowerShell cmdlet:

Start-ADSyncSyncCycle -PolicyType Delta

The -PolicyType Delta option triggers a delta synchronization, which updates changes made since the last synchronization cycle. The -PolicyType Initial option, as suggested in the proposed solution, would initiate an initial synchronization, but it might take some time to complete and is not immediate.

Therefore, the correct response is:

B. No

10) Correct answer: B

On a server with Azure AD Connect installed, navigate to the Start menu and select AD Connect, then Synchronization Service.

1. Go to CONNECTORS tab.

2. Select RUN on the ACTIONS pane.

The proposed solution, involving using Active Directory Sites and Services to force replication of the Global Catalog on a domain controller, does not meet the goal of replicating a new user account's information to Azure AD immediately.

In a scenario with Azure AD configured for hybrid coexistence, the synchronization between on-premises Active Directory and Azure AD is typically managed by Azure AD Connect, not directly through Active Directory Sites and Services.

To synchronize a new user account immediately, you should use the Azure AD Connect server and run the following PowerShell cmdlet:

Start-ADSyncSyncCycle -PolicyType Delta

This initiates a delta synchronization, updating changes made since the last synchronization cycle and effectively replicating the new user account's information to Azure AD. Therefore, the correct response is:

B. No

11) Correct answer: B

Restarting the NetLogon service on a domain controller is not the appropriate action to replicate user information from the on-premise Active Directory to Azure AD immediately, especially in a scenario with Azure AD configured for hybrid coexistence.

To replicate user information to Azure AD promptly, you should use the Azure AD Connect server and run the following PowerShell cmdlet:

Start-ADSyncSyncCycle -PolicyType Delta

This cmdlet initiates a delta synchronization, updating changes made since the last synchronization cycle and effectively replicating the new user account's information to Azure AD.

If you need to manually run a sync cycle, then from PowerShell run Start-ADSyncSyncCycle -PolicyType Delta.

To initiate a full sync cycle, run Start-ADSyncSyncCycle -PolicyType Initial from a PowerShell prompt.

Running a full sync cycle can be very time consuming, so if you need to replicate the user information to Azure AD immediately then run Start-ADSyncSyncCycle -PolicyType Delta.

Reference:

https://docs.microsoft.com/en-us/azure/active-directory/hybrid/how-to-connect-sync-feature-scheduler

12) Correct answer: B

(A: "data will be available to be read-only if Microsoft initiates a failure", so it's not RO if it's not failed-over)

Geo-redundant storage (GRS)

As I explained above it helps us in replicating our data to another region which is far away hundreds of miles away from the primary region. It provides at least 99.99999999999999% (16 9's) durability of objects over a given year. GRS replicates our data to another region, but data will be available to be read-only if Microsoft initiates a failure from primary to the secondary region.

Read-access geo-redundant storage (RA-GRS)

It is based on the GRS, but it also provides an option to read from the secondary region, regardless of whether Microsoft initiates a failover from the primary to the secondary region.

Reference:

https://docs.microsoft.com/en-us/azure/storage/common/storage-redundancy#read-access-to-data-in-the-secondary-region

13) Correct answer: B

Accessing the Virtual Machine blade will not allow you to review the ARM template used by Jon Ross for deploying the virtual machine and the additional Azure Storage account. The ARM template used for deployment is a separate configuration that defines the resources to be provisioned.

To review the ARM template, you should typically look for it in the Azure portal under the "Templates" section or access it through Azure PowerShell or Azure CLI. The ARM template is not directly associated with the Virtual Machine blade.

Answer is No, as questions talk about VM and storage account both which can only be reviewed at RG level.

You should use the Resource Group blade

Reference:

https://docs.microsoft.com/en-us/azure/azure-resource-manager/resource-manager-export-template

14) Correct answer: A

From Resource Group choose ----> Deployments blade

accessing the Resource Group blade can meet the goal of reviewing the ARM template used by Jon Ross to deploy the virtual machine and additional Azure Storage account.

In the Resource Group blade, you can select the resource group where the virtual machine and additional storage account were deployed, and then click on the "Deployments" tab. This will display a list of all deployments made to the resource group, including the ARM template used for the deployment.

Therefore, the solution of accessing the Resource Group blade meets the goal of reviewing the ARM template used by Jon Ross.

Reference:

https://docs.microsoft.com/en-us/azure/azure-resource-

manager/resource-manager-export-
template

15) Correct answer: B

Accessing the Container blade will not
provide you with the ARM template used by
Jon Ross for deploying the virtual machine
and the additional Azure Storage account.
The Container blade is specific to the Blob
container within the storage account, and it
does not give direct access to the ARM
template configuration.

To review the ARM template, you should
typically look for it in the Azure portal under
the "Templates" section or access it through
Azure PowerShell or Azure CLI. The ARM
template is a separate configuration that
defines the resources to be provisioned and
is not directly associated with the Container
blade. Therefore, the correct option is:

B. No

16) Correct answer: C

Stop all the VMs in the availability set. Click Resource groups > your resource group > Resources > your availability set > Virtual Machines > your virtual machine > Stop.

After all the VMs stop, resize the desired VM to a larger size.

Select the resized VM and click Start, and then start each of the stopped VMs.

If the VM you wish to resize is part of an availability set, then you must stop all VMs in the availability set before changing the size of any VM in the availability set.

The reason all VMs in the availability set must be stopped before performing the resize operation to a size that requires different hardware is that all running VMs in the availability set must be using the same physical hardware cluster. Therefore, if a change of physical hardware cluster is required to change the VM size then all VMs must be first stopped and then restarted one-by-one to a different physical hardware cluster.

Reference:

https://azure.microsoft.com/es-es/blog/resize-virtual-machines/

17) Correct answer: C

C. Detach the data disk.

To minimize downtime when attaching a data disk from one Azure virtual machine (VM) to another, the recommended first action is to detach the data disk from the original VM. This allows you to prepare the disk for attachment to the new VM without affecting the operation of the original VM.

Once the data disk is detached, you can then attach it to the target VM, and the downtime for both VMs will be minimized.

Therefore, the correct action is:

C. Detach the data disk.

You can simply detach a data disk from one VM and attach it to the other VM without stopping either of the VMs.

Reference:

https://learn.microsoft.com/en-us/azure/virtual-machines/windows/detach-disk

18) Correct answer: D

To ensure that as many Azure virtual machines (VMs) as possible remain accessible in the event of fabric failure or maintenance, you should set the platformFaultDomainCount property to its maximum value. This setting helps distribute the VMs across fault domains within the Azure datacenter, providing better resilience to failures at the fabric level.

2 or 3 is max for a region so answer is Max.

You can set the parameter --platform-fault-domain-count to 1, 2, or 3 (default of 3 if not specified).

And as described here:

https://docs.microsoft.com/en-us/azure/virtual-machines/availability-set-overview

Each virtual machine in your availability set is assigned an update domain and a fault domain by the underlying Azure platform. Each availability set can be configured with up to three fault domains and twenty update domains.

So, answer is D Max Value

Reference:

https://stackoverflow.com/questions/49779604/how-to-find-maximum-update-domains-fault-domains-available-in-an-azure-region

https://docs.microsoft.com/en-us/azure/virtual-machine-scale-sets/virtual-machine-scale-sets-manage-fault-domains https://docs.microsoft.com/en-us/azure/virtual-machines/windows/manage-availability

19) Correct answer: B

For the platformUpdateDomainCount property in an Azure availability set, the maximum allowed value is 20. The platformUpdateDomainCount property defines the number of update domains used by the platform during maintenance activities. A higher value for platformUpdateDomainCount ensures that VMs in the availability set are distributed across a larger number of update domains, providing better resilience to planned maintenance events.

Therefore, the recommended value to configure for the platformUpdateDomainCount property is:

B. 20

'Each virtual machine in your availability set is assigned an update domain and a fault domain by the underlying Azure platform. Each availability set can be configured with up to three fault domains and twenty update domains.'

Reference:

https://docs.microsoft.com/en-us/azure/virtual-machines/availability-set-overview

20) Correct answer: a, d

Key vault + access policy

To achieve the goal of referencing an administrative password in an Azure Resource Manager (ARM) template without storing it in plain text, you can use an Azure Key Vault. Here's the explanation for the selected options:

An Azure Key Vault (a):

Azure Key Vault allows you to securely store and manage sensitive information such as passwords, secrets, encryption keys, and certificates.

In this scenario, you can store the administrative password securely in the Azure Key Vault and reference it in the ARM template. This way, the password is not stored in plain text within the template.

An Access Policy (d):

Within Azure Key Vault, you can define access policies to control who can access and manage the stored secrets.

By creating an access policy, you can grant the necessary permissions to the services or users that need to retrieve the administrative password from the Azure Key Vault.

In summary, using Azure Key Vault with an access policy allows you to securely store and manage sensitive information, ensuring that the password is not exposed in plain text in the ARM template.

But please note that now the access policy is considered a legacy way to provide access to the key vault. Now you can use RBAC.

Reference:

https://learn.microsoft.com/en-us/azure/key-vault/general/rbac-access-policy

https://learn.microsoft.com/en-us/azure/key-vault/general/assign-access-policy?tabs=azure-portal

21) Correct answer: A

After Windows is installed but before the logon screen appears, Windows Setup searches for the SetupComplete.cmd file in the %WINDIR%\Setup\Scripts\ directory

After you deploy a Virtual Machine you typically need to make some changes before it's ready to use. This is something you can do manually or you could use Remote PowerShell to automate the configuration of your VM after deployment for example.

But now there's a third alternative available allowing you customize your VM: the CustomScriptextension.

This CustomScript extension is executed by the VM Agent and it's very straightforward: you specify which files it needs to download from your storage account and which file it needs to execute. You can even specify arguments that need to be passed to the script. The only requirement is that you execute a .ps1 file.

Reference:
https://docs.microsoft.com/en-us/windows-hardware/manufacture/desktop/add-a-custom-script-to-windows-setup

https://azure.microsoft.com/en-us/blog/automating-vm-customization-tasks-using-custom-script-extension/

https://docs.microsoft.com/en-us/windows-hardware/manufacture/desktop/add-a-custom-script-to-windows-setup

22) Correct answer: B

"New-AzVM" is for creating new VMs, not uploading images.

"Add-AzImage" does not exist. the correct command is "New-AzImage".

"Add-AzImageDataDisk" Adds a data disk to an image object.

"Add-AzVhd" seems to be the correct option, sing the it "Uploads a virtual hard disk from an on-premises machine to Azure (managed disk or blob)."

Example for how you do this:

Add-AzVhd -ResourceGroupName $resourceGroup -Destination $urlOfUploadedImageVhd `

-LocalFilePath $localPath

Reference:

https://docs.microsoft.com/en-us/powershell/module/az.compute/add-azvhd?view=azps-8.3.0

23) For physical servers

- Storage Account

- Azure Recovery Services Vault

- Replication policy

https://docs.microsoft.com/en-us/azure/site-recovery/physical-azure-disaster-recovery

For Hyper-v server

- Hyper-V site

- Azure Recovery Services Vault

- Replication policy

https://docs.microsoft.com/en-nz/azure/site-recovery/hyper-v-prepare-on-premises-tutorial

Azure Recovery Services Vault (c): This is a key component for Azure Site Recovery (ASR), which is used to replicate and protect virtual machines. The Azure Recovery Services Vault manages the replication and recovery settings.

Storage Account (b): Azure Storage is used to store the replicated data. A Storage Account provides the necessary storage resources for holding the replicated VM data.

Replication Policy (e): Replication policies define how often data is replicated, how many recovery points are retained, and other settings related to the replication process. This is crucial for determining the replication behavior for VM1.

The other options are not directly related to Hyper-V VM replication to Azure:

Hyper-V Site (a): Hyper-V Site is not a direct object used for replication. The site in this context typically refers to the Hyper-V site on-premises.

Azure Traffic Manager Instance (d): Azure Traffic Manager is used for distributing network traffic across different Azure regions, but it is not directly related to VM replication.

Endpoint (f): In the context of Azure VM replication, an endpoint typically refers to the configuration that defines how traffic is directed to the replicated VM during failover. While important for the failover process, it's not something you create independently but configure as part of the replication settings.

24) Correct answer: B

"After configuring virtual network peering between VirtualNetworkA and VirtualNetworkB, you confirm that you are able to access VirtualNetworkB from the company's on-premises network." This indicates the Allow/Use gateway transit is set up working. The next step will be restart/reinstall the VPN-Client config at the windows 10 WS.

If you make a change to the topology of your network and have Windows VPN clients, the VPN client package for Windows clients must be downloaded and installed again in order for the changes to be applied to the client.

Choosing the "Allow gateway transit" setting on VirtualNetworkA does not directly address the issue of establishing a connection to VirtualNetworkB from the Windows 10 workstation. The "Allow gateway transit" setting is related to allowing traffic to flow through the gateway of the peered virtual network.

To enable the Windows 10 workstation to establish a connection to VirtualNetworkB, you would typically need to configure peering between VirtualNetworkA and

VirtualNetworkB and ensure that the necessary routing is in place to allow traffic from the Windows 10 workstation to reach VirtualNetworkB. The "Allow gateway transit" setting may not be directly related to resolving this particular connectivity issue.

Reference:

https://docs.microsoft.com/en-us/azure/vpn-gateway/vpn-gateway-about-point-to-site-routing

25) Correct answer: B

No, the solution does not meet the goal.

The "Allow gateway transit" setting is used in the context of virtual network peering to allow traffic to flow through the gateway of the peered virtual network. However, it's important to note that the setting should be applied on the virtual network that contains the gateway, not on the virtual network where the traffic is originating.

In this scenario, since the issue is related to the Windows 10 workstation trying to establish a connection to VirtualNetworkB, you should focus on the peering settings and potentially the Point-to-Site (P2S) VPN configuration. Enabling "Allow gateway transit" on VirtualNetworkB may not address the specific connectivity issue from the Windows 10 workstation.

The correct answer is:

B. No

After reconfiguring \ creating peering existing point-to-site VPN connections need to be recreated.

Reference:

https://docs.microsoft.com/en-us/azure/vpn-gateway/vpn-gateway-about-point-to-site-routing

26) Correct answer: A

"If you make a change to the topology of your network and have Windows VPN clients, the VPN client package for Windows clients must be downloaded and installed again in order for the changes to be applied to the client."

Reference:

https://docs.microsoft.com/en-us/azure/vpn-gateway/vpn-gateway-about-point-to-site-routing

27) Correct answer: C

To provide access for remote workers to the VMs hosted in Microsoft Azure's VNet1, you should:

C. Configure a Point-to-Site (P2S) VPN.

A Point-to-Site VPN allows individual remote users to connect securely to the Azure virtual network over the internet. This is suitable for scenarios where you have a limited number of users who need access to the resources in the Azure virtual network.

S2S would be better if you know that the remote workers work from one location, but we don't know that. They could be working from different locations (like home) that's why P2S is better.

Reference:

https://docs.microsoft.com/en-us/azure/vpn-gateway/work-remotely-support

28) Correct answer: B

No, the solution does not meet the goal.

For a Microsoft SQL Server Always On availability group, the commonly used protocol is TCP, not HTTP. Creating an HTTP health probe on port 1433 is not the correct approach for monitoring SQL Server availability.

To properly configure an Azure internal load balancer as a listener for a SQL Server Always On availability group, you should create a TCP health probe on port 1433, which is the default port for SQL Server. This will ensure that the health probe accurately checks the availability of the SQL Server service.

The correct answer is:

B. No

29) Correct answer: B

No, the solution does not meet the goal.

Setting session persistence to Client IP is not the correct approach for configuring an Azure internal load balancer as a listener for a Microsoft SQL Server Always On availability group.

For SQL Server Always On availability groups, the recommended approach is to use a TCP health probe on port 1433 (the default SQL Server port). This ensures that the load balancer accurately monitors the availability of the SQL Server service without relying on session persistence.

The correct answer is:

B. No

FYI: Session persistence ensures that a client will remain connected to the same server throughout a session or period of time. Because load balancing may, by default, send users to unique servers each time they connect, this can mean that complicated or repeated requests are slowed down.

Reference:

https://docs.microsoft.com/en-us/azure/virtual-machines/windows/sql/virtual-machines-windows-portal-sql-alwayson-int-listener

30) Correct answer: A

Yes, enabling Floating IP on the Azure internal load balancer as a listener for the availability group can meet the goal. By enabling Floating IP, the load balancer will use a floating IP address as the source IP address for outbound flows from the backend pool. This will ensure that the IP address used by the backend pool remains the same even if a VM is restarted or replaced, which is important for maintaining the listener for the availability group.

The solution meets the goal.

Enabling Floating IP is a valid approach when configuring an Azure internal load balancer as a listener for a Microsoft SQL Server Always On availability group. When Floating IP is enabled, it allows the load-balanced IP address to move between the nodes of the availability group as needed.

This capability is important for maintaining connectivity to the SQL Server availability group listener, even if the underlying nodes experience a failover or change in their IP addresses. Floating IP ensures that the load balancer redirects traffic to the correct node hosting the primary replica of the availability group.

Therefore, the correct answer is:

A. Yes

31) Correct answer: E

To configure the two VMs with static internal IP addresses in Azure, you should use the Set-AzureStaticVNetIP PowerShell cmdlet. This cmdlet allows you to set static IP addresses for the virtual network configuration.

Therefore, the correct answer is:

E. Run the Set-AzureStaticVNetIP PowerShell cmdlet.

FYI: For the new PowerShell cmdlets you would use: Set-AzNetworkInterface

The Set-AzureStaticVNetIP PowerShell cmdlet is used to set a static internal IP address for an Azure virtual machine. This cmdlet allows you to set the IP address, subnet mask, and default gateway for the virtual machine's network interface.

Option A, New-AzureRMVMConfig, is used to create a new virtual machine configuration object.

Option B, Set-AzureSubnet, is used to modify the properties of an existing Azure subnet, not to set static IP addresses for virtual machines.

Option C, modifying VM properties in the Azure Management Portal, does not provide a way to set static IP addresses for virtual machines.

Option D, modifying the IP properties in Windows Network and Sharing Center, only applies to the local network interface of the VM and does not set a static internal IP address for the VM on the Azure virtual network.

32) Correct answer: A

Each virtual machine (VM) in Azure can have multiple network interfaces, but for the described configuration, where each VM needs both a public and private IP address, a single network interface per VM is sufficient. Therefore, with five VMs, you would need five network interfaces.

So, the least amount of network interfaces needed for this configuration is 5 (Option A).

5 VM so 5 NIC Cards. We have public and private IP address set to them. However, they need same inbound and outbound rule so create NSG and attach to NIC and this req can be fulfilled 5 NIC hence 5 is right answer.

33) Correct answer: D

Azure Network Security Groups (NSGs) are used to control inbound and outbound traffic to network interfaces (NIC), VMs, and subnets. In this scenario, since the inbound and outbound security rules must be identical for all the virtual machines (VMs) in the same subnet, you can achieve this with a single Network Security Group applied to the subnet.

Therefore, the least amount of security groups needed for this configuration is 1 (Option D).

All identical security groups so you will only require 1 security group as all the settings are the same.

34) Correct answer: B

B. You can recover the files to any VM within the company's subscription.

Azure Backup Instant Restore allows you to recover files and folders from a backed-up virtual machine to any other virtual machine within the same subscription. This means you have flexibility in choosing the destination VM for the file recovery, and you are not limited to restoring files only to the original or infected VM.

Reference:

https://docs.microsoft.com/en-us/azure/backup/backup-azure-restore-windows-server

35) Correct answer: C

The correct answer is:

C. You should restore the VM to a new Azure VM.

When a VM becomes infected with ransomware, it's generally not advisable to simply restore it in place, as the malware might persist. Restoring to a new VM ensures a clean environment and reduces the risk of re-infection.

Therefore, you should restore the VM to a new Azure VM (Option C).

A - If you delete the VM you cannot recover to that VM it must exist.

B - You do not know the other VMs.

C - Creating a New VM you can recover the VM.

D - You can recover from the backup.

Reference:

https://docs.microsoft.com/en-us/azure/backup/backup-azure-arm-restore-vms

36) Correct answer: B

To diagnose and analyze performance issues on the Azure infrastructure, you should use:

B. Azure Monitor

Azure Monitor is the tool designed to collect, analyze, and act on telemetry data from Azure resources. It provides a comprehensive solution for collecting, analyzing, and acting on telemetry data from Azure and non-Azure resources. This includes performance metrics, activity logs, and other types of telemetry.

Azure Traffic Analytics (Option A) is more focused on network traffic analysis, and

Azure Advisor (Option D) provides best practices and recommendations rather than detailed performance monitoring. Azure Activity Log (Option C) primarily logs operations on resources and might not be as suitable for in-depth performance analysis.

Reference:

https://docs.microsoft.com/en-us/azure/azure-monitor/platform/data-platform

37) Correct Answer: ABCDE

Azure Backup supports backup of 64-bit Windows server operating system from Windows Server 2008.

Azure Backup supports backup of 64-bit Windows 10 operating system.

Azure Backup supports backup of 64-bit Debian operating system from Debian 7.9+.

Azure Backup supports backup of VM that are shutdown or offline.

Reference:

https://docs.microsoft.com/en-us/azure/backup/backup-support-matrix-iaas

https://docs.microsoft.com/en-us/azure/virtual-machines/linux/endorsed-distros

38) Correct answer: B

B. No

While the New-AzureADUser cmdlet can be used to create user accounts in Azure AD, it is not designed for creating guest user accounts specifically. To invite external users as guests in Azure AD, you typically use the New-AzureADMSInvitation cmdlet or the Azure portal.

So, the correct approach for the scenario described would be to use the New-

AzureADMSInvitation cmdlet to invite external users as guests in Azure AD.

The New-AzureADUser cmdlet creates a user in Azure Active Directory (Azure AD).

Instead use the New-AzureADMSInvitation cmdlet which is used to invite a new external user to your directory.

Reference:

https://docs.microsoft.com/en-us/powershell/module/azuread/new-azureadmsinvitation

39) Correct answer: B

"Bulk Create" is for new Azure AD Users.

For Guests:

- Use "Bulk invite users" to prepare a comma-separated value (.csv) file with the user information and invitation preferences

- Upload the .csv file to Azure AD

- Verify the users were added to the directory

Instead use the New-AzureADMSInvitation cmdlet which is used to invite a new external user to your directory.

Reference:

https://docs.microsoft.com/en-us/powershell/module/azuread/new-azureadmsinvitation

40) Correct answer: A

A. Yes

Using a PowerShell script with the New-AzureADMSInvitation cmdlet is a suitable solution for inviting external users as guests in Azure AD. This cmdlet is specifically designed for inviting external users to your Azure AD tenant. Each invocation of the cmdlet sends an invitation to one external user, and by scripting the process, you can efficiently invite multiple users from a CSV file.

Therefore, choosing the solution of creating a PowerShell script that runs the New-AzureADMSInvitation cmdlet for each external user meets the goal.

Reference:

https://docs.microsoft.com/en-us/powershell/module/azuread/new-azureadmsinvitation

41) 1) b, 2) b

There is something that we all seem to be forgetting here, and that is that Azure RBAC roles can be applied at three different scopes...management group, subscription, resource group and finally resource. So, LB1 and LB2 are resources that we want the Network Contributor role to manage, which by the way satisfies the principle of least privilege. When you apply the scope to the resource group, then it is applied to all the resources in the resource group which is not what we want. The question specifically referred to LB1 and LB2. These resources are atomic, therefore applying the scope to the two will affect just those two resources.

The Network Contributor role lets you manage networks, but not access them.

Reference:

https://docs.microsoft.com/en-us/azure/role-based-access-control/built-in-roles

42) Correct answer: B

B. From contoso.com, create an OAuth 2.0 authorization endpoint.

To grant access to Azure Kubernetes Service to users in your Azure Active Directory tenant, you need to create an OAuth 2.0 authorization endpoint in your tenant. The endpoint will allow users in your tenant to authenticate and obtain an access token, which can be used to access the Kubernetes API server. Therefore, the first step in this scenario would be to create the OAuth 2.0 authorization endpoint in contoso.com. Option A, modifying the organization relationships settings, is not related to granting access to AKS1. Option C, recreating AKS1, is not necessary as the issue is related to user access. Option D, creating a namespace, is not related to granting access to AKS1 either.

Reference:

https://kubernetes.io/docs/reference/acces s-authn-authz/authentication/

43) Correct answer: AC

Only O365 groups support automatic deletion after 180 days.

A. Microsoft 365 group with Assigned membership type:

Assigned membership type allows manual addition or removal of members by administrators.

This group type is suitable when you want direct control over who is a member of the group, and membership is not automatically managed based on dynamic criteria.

Administrators can add or remove users as needed.

C. Microsoft 365 group with Dynamic User membership type:

Dynamic User membership type allows you to define rules or queries based on user attributes (such as department, job title, etc.), and members are automatically added or removed based on these rules.

This group type is suitable when you want membership to be dynamically managed based on specific criteria.

Memberships are automatically updated as user attributes change.

You can set expiration policy only for Office 365 groups in Azure Active Directory (Azure AD).

Note: With the increase in usage of Office 365 Groups, administrators and users need a way to clean up unused groups. Expiration policies can help remove inactive groups from the system and make things cleaner.

When a group expires, all of its associated services (the mailbox, Planner, SharePoint site, etc.) are also deleted.

You can set up a rule for dynamic membership on security groups or Office 365 groups.

Incorrect Answers:

B, D, E: You can set expiration policy only for Office 365 groups in Azure Active Directory (Azure AD).

Reference:

https://docs.microsoft.com/en-us/office365/admin/create-groups/office-365-groups-expiration-policy?view=o365-worldwide

44) Correct answer: 1) No, 2) No, 3) No

Tested in lab

Correct Answers:

User3 can perform an access review of User1 = No

User1 is a member and not a Guest Account, Access Review specified Guests only.

User3 can perform an access review of UserA = No

User1 is a member and not a Guest Account, Access Review specified Guests only.

User3 can perform an access review of UserB = No

Created Group 1 and Group 2, added Group 2 as a member in Group 1,

Added guest Accounts to Group 1 and Group 2,

In the Access Review results only the Guest Accounts in Group 1 appeared for review and "Not" the Guest accounts in Group 2.

Access to groups and applications for employees and guests changes over time. To reduce the risk associated with stale access assignments, administrators can use Azure Active Directory (Azure AD) to create access reviews for group members or application access. If you need to routinely review access, you can also create recurring access reviews.

Review1 reviews access for guest users who are member of Group1. The group owner is specified as the reviewer.

User3 is the owner of Group1. User2 is the only guest user in Group1.

Note: Dynamic groups and nested groups are not supported with the Access review process.

Reference:

Create an access review of groups and applications in Azure AD access reviews:

https://docs.microsoft.com/en-us/azure/active-directory/governance/create-access-review

45) Correct answer: 1) No, 2) No, 3) No

Subscription should be moved by can't be added to 2 groups.

- NO: Subscription 1: is not allowed to create a VNET.

- NO: Subscription 2: Allowed to create a VNET which restricts anything else.

It's because of the "Allowed Resources Policy". You can only create resources of the allowed type and the ones which cannot be assigned tags.

TR ->MG11 -> MG21 - Sub1

->MG12 - sub2

- NO: Subscription 1: already in one Management group called 21, so cannot add into another. A Subscription can be assigned to 1 Management Group.

46) Correct answer: B

You are prevented from creating Azure SQL servers anywhere in Subscription 1, except from ContosoRG1. There's an Exclusion on ContosoRG1.

Not allowed resource types (Deny): Prevents a list of resource types from being deployed.

Exclusions and RG1 is there.

Reference:

https://docs.microsoft.com/en-us/azure/governance/policy/overview#policy-definition

47) VNET1 will only have Department: D1 tag & VNET 2 will only have Label: Value1 tag

Remediation task is needed to assign new tags to already existing resources (VNET1 existed before Policy was assigned), therefore VNET1 has no tags from the policy assigned.

This would be the case if a remediation task has been performed on the policy assignment, but this was not mentioned in the question.

Reference:

https://learn.microsoft.com/en-us/azure/azure-resource-manager/management/tag-policies

48) Correct answer: C

All of them. Moving a resource only moves it to a new Resource Group or Subscription. It doesn't change the location of the resource.

You can move a VM and its associated resources to a different subscription by using the Azure portal.

You can now move an Azure Recovery Service (ASR) Vault to either a new resource group within the current subscription or to a new subscription.

Reference:

https://docs.microsoft.com/en-us/azure/azure-resource-manager/management/move-support-resources

https://docs.microsoft.com/en-us/azure/azure-resource-manager/management/move-support-resources#microsoftcompute

https://docs.microsoft.com/en-us/azure/azure-resource-manager/management/move-support-resources#microsoftnetwork

https://docs.microsoft.com/en-us/azure/azure-resource-manager/management/move-support-resources#microsoftstorage

https://docs.microsoft.com/en-us/azure/azure-resource-

manager/management/move-support-
resources#microsoftrecoveryservices

49) Correct answer: C

To resolve the issue and ensure that
Admin1 can deploy the Marketplace
resource successfully, you should take the
following steps:

C. From Azure PowerShell, run the Set-
AzMarketplaceTerms cmdlet

Explanation:

The error message indicates that legal
terms for the Marketplace item have not
been accepted.

The Set-AzMarketplaceTerms cmdlet is
used to accept the terms for a Marketplace
item in a programmatic way through
PowerShell.

Running this cmdlet allows the user to
programmatically accept the legal terms,
enabling them to deploy the Marketplace
resource without encountering the
validation error.

Please note that assigning the Billing administrator role (Option D) is related to billing permissions but may not address the specific issue mentioned in the error message. The Set-AzMarketplaceTerms cmdlet is designed for handling legal terms acceptance for Marketplace items.

Set-AzMarketplaceTerms -Publisher <String> -Product <String> -Name <String> [-Accept] [-Terms <PSAgreementTerms>] [-DefaultProfile <IAzureContextContainer>] [-WhatIf] [-Confirm] [<CommonParameters>]

Reference:

https://docs.microsoft.com/en-us/powershell/module/Az.MarketplaceOrdering/Set-AzMarketplaceTerms?view=azps-4.6.0

50) Correct answer: B

B. From the Directory role blade, modify the directory role

To assign the User administrator administrative role to AdminUser1, you need to navigate to the "Directory role" blade in the Azure Active Directory (Azure AD) portal.

The User administrator role is a directory role, and you can assign it from the Directory role settings.

Modifying the directory role for AdminUser1 to include the User administrator role will grant the necessary administrative privileges.

Option A is incorrect because assigning a new license is unrelated to granting directory roles.

Option C is incorrect because inviting a user account to a new group does not directly assign directory roles related to administrative privileges.

Active Directory -> Manage Section -> Roles and administrators-> Search for Admin and assign a user to it.

select Active directory --> Users--> select the username --> Assigned roles --> click on +add Assignments --> select User administrator role.

Assign a role to a user -

1. Sign in to the Azure portal with an account that's a global admin or privileged role admin for the directory.

2. Select Azure Active Directory, select Users, and then select a specific user from the list.

3. For the selected user, select Directory role, select Add role, and then pick the appropriate admin roles from the Directory roles list, such as Conditional access administrator.

4. Press Select to save.

Reference:

https://docs.microsoft.com/en-us/azure/active-

directory/fundamentals/active-directory-
users-assign-role-azure-portal

51) Correct answer: A

Active Directory-> Manage Section >
Choose Licenses -> All Products -> Select
Azure Active Directory Premium P2 -> Then
assign a user to it.

Azure AD Premium features are license-
based, and to enable users to utilize these
features, you need to assign the
appropriate licenses to those users. In this
case, you have purchased 10 Azure AD
Premium P2 licenses, and to ensure that 10
users can use all the Azure AD Premium
features, you should assign a license to each
of those users.

Option A, "Assign a license from the
Licenses blade of Azure AD," is the correct
choice because it allows you to assign
specific licenses to individual users or
groups. By going to the Licenses blade in
Azure AD, you can select the Azure AD

Premium P2 license and assign it to the 10 users who need access to the premium features. This action activates the premium features for those users.

Options B, C, and D are not relevant to assigning licenses for enabling Azure AD Premium features. They involve different tasks such as managing user groups, adding enterprise applications, and modifying directory roles, but they do not directly address the licensing aspect needed to activate premium features for specific users.

Reference:

https://docs.microsoft.com/en-us/azure/active-directory/fundamentals/license-users-groups

52) Correct Answer: C

IT Service Management Connector (ITSMC) allows you to connect Azure to a supported

IT Service Management (ITSM) product or service. Azure services like Azure Log Analytics and Azure Monitor provide tools to detect, analyze, and troubleshoot problems with your Azure and non-Azure resources. But the work items related to an issue typically reside in an ITSM product or service. ITSMC provides a bi-directional connection between Azure and ITSM tools to help you resolve issues faster. ITSMC supports connections with the following ITSM tools: ServiceNow, System Center Service Manager, Provance, Cherwell.

Reference:

https://docs.microsoft.com/en-us/azure/azure-monitor/alerts/itsmc-overview

53) Correct answer: A

To grant administrative privileges to a user named admin1@contoso.com on all the computers that will be joined to the Azure

AD domain, you should perform the configuration in Azure AD as follows:

A. Configure device settings from the Devices blade.

Explanation:

Configuring device settings from the Devices blade in Azure AD allows you to manage settings related to device access and administration. By configuring device settings, you can control the administrative privileges that users have on devices joined to the Azure AD domain.

Options B, C, and D involve different configurations:

B. Configuring providers from the MFA Server blade is related to configuring multi-factor authentication (MFA) providers and is not directly relevant to granting administrative privileges on devices.

C. Configuring user settings from the Users blade is more related to user-specific settings and may not be the appropriate place to configure administrative privileges on devices.

D. Configuring general settings from the Groups blade is related to configuring settings for Azure AD groups and may not be the appropriate place for device-specific administrative configurations.

Therefore, the correct choice for granting administrative privileges on all the computers joined to the Azure AD domain is to configure device settings from the Devices blade.

When you connect a Windows device with Azure AD using an Azure AD join, Azure AD adds the following security principles to the local administrators' group on the device:

☞ The Azure AD global administrator role

☞ The Azure AD device administrator role

☞ The user performing the Azure AD join

In the Azure portal, you can manage the device administrator role on the Devices page. To open the Devices page:

1. Sign in to your Azure portal as a global administrator or device administrator.

2. On the left navbar, click Azure Active Directory.

3. In the Manage section, click Devices.

4. On the Devices page, click Device settings.

5. To modify the device administrator role, configure Additional local administrators on Azure AD joined devices.

Reference:

https://docs.microsoft.com/en-us/azure/active-directory/devices/assign-local-admin

54) User1 can add Device2 to Group1: No

User2 can add Device1 to Group1: Yes

User2 can add Device2 to Group2: No

Explanation:

Groups can contain both registered and joined devices as members.

As a global administrator or cloud device administrator, you can manage the registered or joined devices. Intune Service administrators can update and delete devices. User administrator can manage users but not devices.

User1 is a cloud device administrator. Users in this role can enable, disable, and delete devices in Azure AD and read Windows 10 BitLocker keys (if present) in the Azure portal. The role does not grant permissions to manage any other properties on the device.

User2 is the owner of Group1. He can add Device1 to Group1.

Group2 is configured for dynamic membership. The properties on which the membership of a device in a group of the type dynamic device are defined cannot be changed by either an end user or a user administrator. User2 cannot add any device to Group2.

Reference:

https://docs.microsoft.com/en-
us/azure/active-directory/devices/device-
management-azure-portal

55) Correct answer: C

You can't delete a Recovery Services vault
with any of the following dependencies:

- You can't delete a vault that contains
backup data. Once backup data is deleted, it
will go into the soft deleted state.

- You can't delete a vault that contains
backup data in the soft deleted state.

VM's running or not would not block the
deletion of a Resource Group.

Storage Accounts also don't block the
deletion of a Resource Group.

Reference:

https://docs.microsoft.com/en-us/azure/azure-resource-manager/management/delete-resource-group?tabs=azure-powershell#required-access-and-deletion-failures

https://docs.microsoft.com/en-us/azure/backup/backup-azure-delete-vault?tabs=portal#before-you-start

56) Correct answer: B

The User Access Administrator role allows users to manage user access to Azure resources, but it does not provide the ability to assign roles to other users.

The Network Contributor role grants users the ability to manage networks, but it also does not provide the ability to assign roles to other users.

The Security Admin and Security Reader roles are not relevant to the task at hand.

Therefore, the correct option is to assign User1 the User Access Administrator role for VNet1, which will allow them to assign the Reader role to other users for that specific virtual network.

Has full access to all resources including the right to delegate access to others.

Note:

There are several versions of this question in the exam. The question has two possible correct answers:

☞ Assign User1 the User Access Administrator role for VNet1.

☞ Assign User1 the Owner role for VNet1.

Other incorrect answer options you may see on the exam include the following:

☞ Assign User1 the Contributor role for VNet1.

☞ Remove User1 from the Security Reader and Reader roles for Subscription1. Assign User1 the Contributor role for Subscription1.

☞ Remove User1 from the Security Reader role for Subscription1. Assign User1 the Contributor role for RG1.

Reference:

https://docs.microsoft.com/en-us/azure/role-based-access-control/overview

57) Correct answer: A

When you add a custom domain in azure u are not allowed to use that unless u prove its your domain. So, once u add the custom domain name azure asks u to verify and you have to provide some inputs to verify that it's these inputs can be provided in TXT or MX. So, its MX in this case.

To verify your custom domain name (example)

1. Sign in to the Azure portal using a Global administrator account for the directory.

2. Select Azure Active Directory, and then select Custom domain names.

3. On the Fabrikam - Custom domain names page, select the custom domain name, Contoso.

4. On the Contoso page, select Verify to make sure your custom domain is properly registered and is valid for Azure AD. Use either the TXT or the MX record type.

Note:

There are several versions of this question in the exam. The question can have two correct answers:

1. MX

2. TXT

The question can also have other incorrect answer options, including the following:

1. SRV

2. NSEC3

Reference:

https://docs.microsoft.com/en-us/azure/dns/dns-web-sites-custom-domain

58) Correct answer: B

B. No

Explanation:

The DevTest Labs User role is not specific to logic app creation, and assigning this role would not meet the goal of providing the Developers group with the ability to create Azure logic apps in the Dev resource group.

For creating Azure logic apps, you should assign a role that specifically grants the necessary permissions for working with logic apps in a resource group. The appropriate role for this scenario would be the "Logic App Contributor" or "Contributor" role at the resource group level.

Therefore, the correct solution would be to assign the "Logic App Contributor" role or

"Contributor" role to the Developers group on the Dev resource group.

The Azure DevTest Labs is a role used for Azure DevTest Labs, not for Logic Apps.

DevTest Labs User role only lets you connect, start, restart, and shutdown virtual machines in your Azure DevTest Labs.

The Logic App Contributor role lets you manage logic app, but not access to them. It provides access to view, edit, and update a logic app.

Reference:

https://docs.microsoft.com/en-us/azure/role-based-access-control/built-in-roles

https://docs.microsoft.com/en-us/azure/logic-apps/logic-apps-securing-a-logic-app

https://docs.microsoft.com/en-us/azure/role-based-access-control/built-in-roles#devtest-labs-user

59) Correct answer: B

You would need the Logic App Contributor role.

Logic App Operator - Lets you read, enable, and disable logic apps, but not edit or update them.

Logic App Contributor - Lets you create, manage logic apps, but not access to them.

The Logic App Operator role is designed for users who need to view the logic app but should not have the ability to modify or manage it. Assigning the Logic App Operator role to the Developers group would not meet the goal of providing them with the ability to create Azure logic apps in the Dev resource group.

For creating Azure logic apps, you should assign a role that specifically grants the necessary permissions for working with logic apps in a resource group. The appropriate role for this scenario would be the "Logic App Contributor" or "Contributor" role at the resource group level.

Therefore, the correct solution would be to assign the "Logic App Contributor" role or "Contributor" role to the Developers group on the Dev resource group.

Reference:

https://docs.microsoft.com/en-us/azure/role-based-access-control/built-in-roles

https://docs.microsoft.com/en-us/azure/logic-apps/logic-apps-securing-a-logic-app

https://docs.microsoft.com/en-us/azure/role-based-access-control/built-in-roles#logic-app-operator

60) Correct Answer: A

The Contributor role can manage all resources (and add resources) in a Resource Group. Contributor role can create logic apps.

Alternatively, we can use the Logic App Contributor role, which lets you manage logic app, but not access to them. It provides access to view, edit, and update a logic app.

Assigning the Contributor role to the Developers group on the Dev resource group would meet the goal of providing them with the ability to create Azure logic apps in that specific resource group. The Contributor role grants full access to all resources within the resource group, allowing members of the Developers group to create, modify, and delete resources, including Azure logic apps, in the Dev resource group.

Therefore, the solution of assigning the Contributor role to the Developers group on the Dev resource group meets the goal.

Contributor role can create logic apps.

Reference:

https://docs.microsoft.com/en-us/azure/role-based-access-control/built-in-roles#contributor

https://docs.microsoft.com/en-us/azure/role-based-access-control/built-in-roles#logic-app-contributor

End of Practice Test I

Practice Test II

1) DRAG DROP -

You have an Azure subscription that is used by four departments in your company. The subscription contains 10 resource groups. Each department uses resources in several resource groups.

You need to send a report to the finance department. The report must detail the costs for each department.

Which three actions should you perform in sequence?

Select and Place:

Actions:

a) Assign a tag to each resource group.

b) Assign a tag to each resource.

c) Download the usage report.

d) From the cost analysis blade, filter the view by tag.

e) Open the Resource Costs blade of each resource group.

Answer area:

1)..

2)..

3)..

2) You have an Azure subscription named Subscription1 that contains an Azure Log Analytics workspace named Workspace1.

You need to view the error events from a table named Event.

Which query should you run in Workspace1?

A. Get-Event Event | where {$_.EventType == "error"}

B. search in (Event) "error"

C. select * from Event where EventType == "error"

D. search in (Event) * | where EventType -eq "error"

3) HOTSPOT -

You have an Azure subscription that contains a virtual network named VNET1 in the East US 2 region. A network interface named VM1-NI is connected to

VNET1.

You successfully deploy the following Azure Resource Manager template.

```json
{
    "apiVersion": "2017-03-30",
    "type": "Microsoft.Compute/virtualMachines",
    "name": "VM1",
    "zones": "1",
    "location": "EastUS2",
    "dependsOn": [
      "[resourceId('Microsoft.Network/networkInterfaces', 'VM1-NI')]"
    ],
    "properties": {
      "hardwareProfile": {
        "vmSize": "Standard_A2_v2"
      },
      "osProfile": {
        "computerName": "VM1",
        "adminUsername": "AzureAdmin",
        "adminPassword": "[parameters('adminPassword')]"
      },
      "storageProfile": {
        "imageReference": "[variables('image')]",
        "osDisk": {
          "createOption": "FromImage"
        }
      },
      "networkProfile": {
        "networkInterfaces": [
          {
            "id": "[resourceId('Microsoft.Network/networkInterfaces', 'VM1-NI')]"
```

```
        }
      ]
    }
  }
},
{
  "apiVersion": "2017-03-30",
  "type": "Microsoft.Compute/virtualMachines",
  "name": "VM2",
  "zones": "2",
  "location: "EastUS2",
  "dependsOn": [
    "[resourceId('Microsoft.Network/networkInterfaces', 'VM2-NI')]"
  ],
  "properties": {
    "hardwareProfile": {
      "vmSize": "Standard_A2_v2"
    },
    "osProfile": {
      "computerName": "VM2",
      "adminUsername": "AzureAdmin",
      "adminPassword": "[parameters('adminPassword')]"
    },
    "storageProfile": {
      "imageReference": "[variables('image')]",
      "osDisk": {
        "createOption": "FromImage"
      }
    },
    "networkProfile": {
      "networkInterfaces": [
        {
          "id": "[resourceId('Microsoft.Network/networkInterfaces', 'VM2-NI')]"
        }
      ]
    }
  }
}
```

For each of the following statements, choose Yes if the statement is true. Otherwise, select No.

Hot Area:

Answer area:

Statements:

1) VM1 and VM2 can connect to VNET1

2) If an Azure datacenter becomes unavailable, VM1 and VM2 will be available.

3) If the East US 2 region becomes unavailable, VM1 and VM2 will be available.

4) You have an Azure subscription named Subscription1. Subscription1 contains the resource groups in the following table.

Name	Azure region	Policy
RG1	West Europe	Policy1
RG2	North Europe	Policy2
RG3	France Central	Policy3

RG1 has a web app named WebApp1. WebApp1 is located in West Europe. You move WebApp1 to RG2. What is the effect of the move?

A. The App Service plan for WebApp1 remains in West Europe. Policy2 applies to WebApp1.

B. The App Service plan for WebApp1 moves to North Europe. Policy2 applies to WebApp1.

C. The App Service plan for WebApp1 remains in West Europe. Policy1 applies to WebApp1.

D. The App Service plan for WebApp1 moves to North Europe. Policy1 applies to WebApp1.

5) HOTSPOT –

You have an Azure subscription named Subscription1 that has a subscription ID of c276fc76-9cd4-44c9-99a7-4fd71546436e.

You need to create a custom RBAC role named CR1 that meets the following requirements:

☞ Can be assigned only to the resource groups in Subscription1

☞ Prevents the management of the access permissions for the resource groups

☞ Allows the viewing, creating, modifying, and deleting of resources within the resource groups

What should you specify in the assignable scopes and the permission elements of the definition of CR1?

To answer, choose the appropriate options in the answer area.

Hot Area:

Answer Area

"assignableScopes": [

1)

a	"/"
b	"/subscriptions/c276fc76-9cd4-44c9-99a7-4fd71546436e"
c	"/subscriptions/c276fc76-9cd4-44c9-99a7-4fd71546436e/resourceGroups"

```
],
"permissions": [
  {
      "actions": [
        "*"
      ],
      "additionalProperties": {},
      "dataActions": [],
      "notActions": [
```

2)

a	"Microsoft.Authorization/*"
b	"Microsoft.Resources/*"
c	"Microsoft.Security/*"

```
],
"notDataActions": []
  }
],
```

6) You have an Azure subscription.

Users access the resources in the subscription from either home or from customer sites. From home, users must

establish a point-to-site VPN to access the Azure resources. The users on the customer sites access the Azure resources by using site-to-site VPNs.

You have a line-of-business-app named App1 that runs on several Azure virtual machine. The virtual machines run Windows Server 2016.

You need to ensure that the connections to App1 are spread across all the virtual machines.

What are two possible Azure services that you can use?

Each correct answer presents a complete solution.

A. an internal load balancer

B. a public load balancer

C. an Azure Content Delivery Network (CDN)

D. Traffic Manager

E. an Azure Application Gateway

7) You have an Azure subscription.

You have 100 Azure virtual machines.

You need to quickly identify underutilized virtual machines that can have their service tier changed to a less expensive offering.

Which blade should you use?

A. Monitor

B. Advisor

C. Metrics

D. Customer insights

8) HOTSPOT –
You have an Azure Active Directory (Azure AD) tenant.
You need to create a conditional access policy that requires all users to use multi-factor authentication when they access the

Azure portal.
Which three settings should you configure?

Answer Area

* Name

Policy1   ✓

Assignments

Users and groups ⓘ 0 users and groups selected	>
Cloud apps ⓘ 0 cloud apps selected	>
Conditions ⓘ 0 conditions selected	>

Access controls

Grant ⓘ 0 controls selected	>
Session ⓘ	>

9) You have an Azure Active Directory (Azure AD) tenant named contoso.onmicrosoft.com.

The User administrator role is assigned to a user named Admin1.

An external partner has a Microsoft account that uses the user1@outlook.com sign in.

Admin1 attempts to invite the external partner to sign in to the Azure AD tenant and receives the following error message: `Unable to invite user user1@outlook.com `" Generic authorization exception. `

You need to ensure that Admin1 can invite the external partner to sign in to the Azure AD tenant.

What should you do?

A. From the Users settings blade, modify the External collaboration settings.

B. From the Custom domain names blade, add a custom domain.

C. From the Organizational relationships blade, add an identity provider.

D. From the Roles and administrators' blade, assign the Security administrator role to Admin1.

10) You have an Azure subscription linked to an Azure Active Directory tenant. The tenant includes a user account named User1.

You need to ensure that User1 can assign a policy to the tenant root management group.

What should you do?

A. Assign the Owner role for the Azure Subscription to User1, and then modify the default conditional access policies.

B. Assign the Owner role for the Azure subscription to User1, and then instruct User1 to configure access management for Azure resources.

C. Assign the Global administrator role to User1, and then instruct User1 to configure access management for Azure resources.

D. Create a new management group and delegate User1 as the owner of the new management group.

11) HOTSPOT –

You have an Azure Active Directory (Azure AD) tenant named adatum.com. Adatum.com contains the groups in the following table.

Name	Group type	Membership type	Membership rule
Group1	Security	Dynamic user	(user.city –startsWith "m"
Group2	Microsoft 365	Dynamic user	(user.department –notIn ["human resources"])
Group3	Microsoft 365	Assigned	Not applicable

You create two user accounts that are configured as shown in the following table.

Name	City	Department	Office 365 license assigned
User1	Montreal	Human resources	Yes
User2	Melbourne	Marketing	No

Of which groups are User1 and User2 members?

To answer, choose the appropriate options in the answer area.

Hot Area:

Answer Area

User1: ▼

a	Group1 only
b	Group2 only
c	Group3 only
d	Group1 and Group2 only
e	Group1 and Group3 only
f	Group2 and Group3 only
g	Group1, Group2, and Group3

User2: ▼

a	Group1 only
b	Group2 only
c	Group3 only
d	Group1 and Group2 only
e	Group1 and Group3 only
f	Group2 and Group3 only
g	Group1, Group2, and Group3

12) HOTSPOT –

You have a hybrid deployment of Azure Active Directory (Azure AD) that contains the users shown in the following table.

Name	Type	Source
User1	Member	Azure AD
User2	Member	Windows Server Active Directory
User3	Guest	Microsoft account

You need to modify the JobTitle and UsageLocation attributes for the users.

For which users can you modify the attributes from Azure AD? T

o answer, choose the appropriate options in the answer area.

Hot Area:

Answer Area

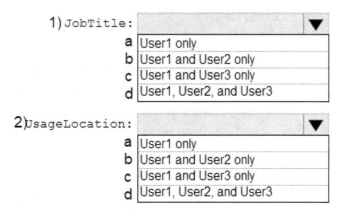

1) JobTitle:
a	User1 only
b	User1 and User2 only
c	User1 and User3 only
d	User1, User2, and User3

2) UsageLocation:
a	User1 only
b	User1 and User2 only
c	User1 and User3 only
d	User1, User2, and User3

13) You need to ensure that an Azure Active Directory (Azure AD) user named Admin1 is assigned the required role to enable Traffic Analytics for an Azure subscription.

Solution: You assign the Network Contributor role at the subscription level to Admin1.

Does this meet the goal?

A. Yes

B. No

14) You need to ensure that an Azure Active Directory (Azure AD) user named Admin1 is assigned the required role to enable Traffic Analytics for an Azure subscription.

Solution: You assign the Owner role at the subscription level to Admin1.

Does this meet the goal?

A. Yes

B. No

15) You need to ensure that an Azure Active Directory (Azure AD) user named Admin1 is assigned the required role to enable Traffic Analytics for an Azure subscription.

Solution: You assign the Reader role at the subscription level to Admin1.

Does this meet the goal?

A. Yes

B. No

16) You have an Azure subscription that contains a user named User1. You need to ensure that User1 can deploy virtual machines and manage virtual networks. The solution must use the principle of least privilege.

Which role-based access control (RBAC) role should you assign to User1?

A. Owner

B. Virtual Machine Contributor

C. Contributor

D. Virtual Machine Administrator Login

17) HOTSPOT -

You have an Azure Active Directory (Azure AD) tenant that contains three global administrators named Admin1, Admin2, and Admin3.

The tenant is associated to an Azure subscription.

Access control for the subscription is configured as shown in the Access control exhibit.

(Click the Access Control tab.)

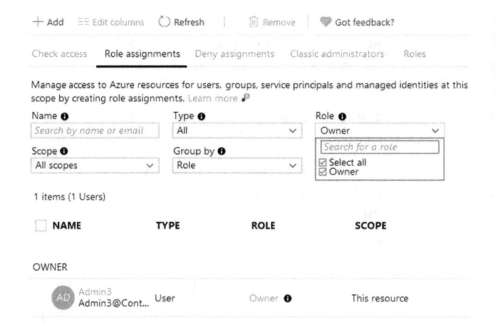

You sign in to the Azure portal as Admin1 and configure the tenant as shown in the Tenant exhibit. (Click the Tenant tab.)

Save ✖ Discard

Directory properties

* Name

| Cont190525outlook | ✓ |

Country or region

Slovenia

Location

EU Model Clause compliant datacenters

Notification language

| English | ⌄ |

Directory ID

| a93d91a6-faca-4fa6-a749-f6c25469152e | 📋 |

Technical contact

| | ✓ |

Global privacy contact

| | ✓ |

Privacy statement URL

| | ✓ |

Access management for Azure resources

Admin1@Cont190525outlook.onmicrosoft.com (Admin1@Cont190525outlook.onmicrosoft.com) can manage access to all Azure subscriptions and management groups in this directory. Learn more

| Yes | No |

For each of the following statements,

167

choose Yes if the statement is true. Otherwise, select No.

Hot Area:

Answer area:

Statements:

1) Admin1 can add Admin 2 as an owner of the subscription.

2) Admin3 can add Admin 2 as an owner of the subscription.

3) Admin2 can create a resource group in the subscription.

18) You have an Azure subscription named Subscription1 that contains an Azure virtual machine named VM1. VM1 is in a resource group named RG1.

VM1 runs services that will be used to deploy resources to RG1.

You need to ensure that a service running

on VM1 can manage the resources in RG1 by using the identity of VM1.

What should you do first?

A. From the Azure portal, modify the Managed Identity settings of VM1

B. From the Azure portal, modify the Access control (IAM) settings of RG1

C. From the Azure portal, modify the Access control (IAM) settings of VM1

D. From the Azure portal, modify the Policies settings of RG1

19) You have an Azure subscription that contains a resource group named TestRG. You use TestRG to validate an Azure deployment.

TestRG contains the following resources:

Name	Type	Description
VM1	Virtual Machine	VM1 is running and configured to back up to Vault1 daily
Vault1	Recovery Services Vault	Vault1 includes all backups of VM1
VNET1	Virtual Network	VNET1 has a resource lock of type Delete

You need to delete TestRG. What should you do first?

A. Modify the backup configurations of VM1 and modify the resource lock type of VNET1

B. Remove the resource lock from VNET1 and delete all data in Vault1

C. Turn off VM1 and remove the resource lock from VNET1

D. Turn off VM1 and delete all data in Vault1

20) You have an Azure DNS zone named adatum.com.

You need to delegate a subdomain named research.adatum.com to a different DNS server in Azure.

What should you do?

A. Create an NS record named research in the adatum.com zone.

B. Create a PTR record named research in the adatum.com zone.

C. Modify the SOA record of adatum.com.

D. Create an A record named *.research in the adatum.com zone.

21) DRAG DROP -

You have an Azure Active Directory (Azure AD) tenant that has the contoso.onmicrosoft.com domain name.

You have a domain name of contoso.com registered at a third-party registrar.

You need to ensure that you can create Azure AD users that have names containing a suffix of @contoso.com.

Which three actions should you perform in sequence? To answer, choose the appropriate actions from the list of actions to the answer area and arrange them in the correct order.

Select and Place:

Actions:

a) Add a record to the public contoso.com DNS zone.

b) Add an Azure AD tenant.

c) Configure company branding.

d) Create an Azure DNS zone.

e) Add a custom name.

f) Verify the domain.

Answer area:

1)...

2)...

3)...

22) In your Azure subscription named Subscription1, you have an Azure Log Analytics workspace named Workspace1. Your goal is to retrieve error events from a table named Event.

Which query should you use in Workspace1?

A. Get-Event Event | where {$_.EventType == "error"}

B. search in (Event) "error"

C. select * from Event where EventType == "error"

D. search in (Event) * | where EventType - eq "error"

23) You have a registered DNS domain called contoso.com, and you've set up a public Azure DNS zone with the same name. Your goal is to make sure that the records you create in the contoso.com Azure DNS zone are accessible from the internet.

What steps should you take?

A. Establish Name Server (NS) records within the contoso.com Azure DNS zone.

B. Update the Start of Authority (SOA) record within the DNS domain registrar for contoso.com.

C. Create the Start of Authority (SOA) record within the contoso.com Azure DNS zone.

D. Modify the Name Server (NS) records within the DNS domain registrar for contoso.com.

24) HOTSPOT –

You have an Azure subscription that

contains a storage account named storage1. The subscription is linked to an Azure Active Directory (Azure AD) tenant named contoso.com that syncs to an on-premises Active Directory domain.

The domain contains the security principals shown in the following table.

Name	Type
User1	User
Computer1	Computer

In Azure AD, you create a user named User2.

The storage1 account contains a file share named share1 and has the following configurations.

```
"kind": "StorageV2",
"properties": {
                "azureFilesIdentityBasedAuthentication": {
                    "directoryServiceOptions": "AD",
                    "activeDirectoryProperties": {
                        "domainName": "Contoso.com",
                        "netBiosDomainName": "Contoso.com",
                        "forestName": "Contoso.com",

                }
        }
```

For each of the following statements, choose Yes if the statement is true. Otherwise, select No.

Hot Area:

Answer area:

Statements:

1) You can assign the storage file Data SMB Share Contributor role to user1 for share1.

2) You can assign the storage file Data SMB Share Reader role to Computer1 for share1.

3) You can assign the storage file Data SMB Share Elevated Contributor role to user2 for share1.

25) HOTSPOT –

You have an Azure subscription named Subscription1 that contains a virtual network VNet1.

You add the users in the following table.

User	Role
User1	Owner
User2	Security Admin
User3	Network Contributor

Which user can perform each configuration?

Hot Area:

Answer Area

Add a subnet to VNet1:

User1 only
User3 only
User1 and User3 only
User2 and User3 only
User1, User2, and User3

Assign a user the Reader role to VNet1:

User1 only
User2 only
User3 only
User1 and User2 only
User2 and User3 only
User1, User2, and User3

26) HOTSPOT –

You have the Azure resources shown on the following exhibit.

Tenant Root Group

MG1

Sub1

RG1

VM1

You plan to track resource usage and prevent the deletion of resources. To which resources can you apply locks and tags?

To answer, select the appropriate options in the answer area.

Hot Area:

Answer Area

Locks:

RG1 and VM1 only
Sub1 and RG1 only
Sub1, RG1, and VM1 only
MG1, Sub1, RG1, and VM1 only
Tenant Root Group, MG1, Sub1, RG1, and VM1

Tags:

RG1 and VM1 only
Sub1 and RG1 only
Sub1, RG1, and VM1 only
MG1, Sub1, RG1, and VM1 only
Tenant Root Group, MG1, Sub1, RG1, and VM1

27) In your Azure Active Directory (Azure AD) tenant, you intend to perform bulk user deletion using the Bulk delete feature in the Azure Active Directory admin center. To achieve this, you need to create and upload a file specifying the users to be deleted.

180

Which user attributes should be included in the file?

A. Include only the user's principal name and usage location of each user.

B. Include only the user's principal name of each user.

C. Include only the display name of each user.

D. Include only the display name and usage location of each user.

E. Include only the display name and user principal name of each user.

28) HOTSPOT –

You have an Azure subscription named Sub1 that contains the Azure resources shown in the following table.

181

Name	Type
RG1	Resource group
storage1	Storage account
VNET1	Virtual network

You assign an Azure policy that has the following settings:

↪ Scope: Sub1

↪ Exclusions: Sub1/RG1/VNET1

↪ Policy definition: Append a tag and its value to resources

↪ Policy enforcement: Enabled

↪ Tag name: Tag4

↪ Tag value: value4

You assign tags to the resources as shown in the following table.

Resource	Tag
Sub1	Tag1:subscription
RG1	Tag2:IT
storage1	Tag3:value1
VNET1	Tag3:value2

For each of the following statements, select Yes if the statement is true. Otherwise, select No.

Hot Area:

Answer area:

Statements:

1) RG1 has the Tag2:IT tag assigned only.

2) Storage1 has the Tag1:Subscription, Tag2:IT, Tag3:value1, and Tag4:value4 tags assigned

3) VNET1 has the Tag2:IT and Tag3:value2 tags assigned only.

29) You need to ensure that an Azure Active Directory (Azure AD) user named Admin1 is assigned the required role to enable Traffic Analytics for an Azure subscription.

Solution: You assign the Traffic Manager Contributor role at the subscription level to Admin1.

Does this meet the goal?

A. Yes

B. No

30) You have three offices and an Azure subscription that contains an Azure Active Directory (Azure AD) tenant. You need to grant user management permissions to a local administrator in each office.

What should you use?

A. Azure AD roles

B. Administrative units

C. Access packages in Azure AD entitlement management

D. Azure roles

31) You have an Azure Directory (Azure AD) tenant named Adatum and an Azure Subscription named Subscription1. Adatum contains a group named Developers.

Subscription1 contains a resource group named Dev.

You need to provide the Developers group with the ability to create Azure logic apps in the Dev resource group.

Solution: On Dev, you assign the Logic App Contributor role to the Developers group.

Does this meet the goal?

A. Yes

B. No

32) HOTSPOT –

You have an Azure Load Balancer named LB1.

You assign a user named User1 the roles shown in the following exhibit.

User1 assignments – LB1

Assignments for the selected user, group, service principal, or managed identity at this scope or inherited to this scope.

| Search by assignment name or description |

Role assignments (2) ⓘ

Role	D..	Scope	Group assignment
User Access Administrator	L...	This resource	- -
Virtual Machine Contributor	L...	Resource group (inherited)	- -

Choose the answer choice that completes each statement based on the information presented in the graphic.

Hot Area:

Answer Area

User1 can **[answer choice]** LB1.

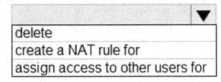

delete
create a NAT rule for
assign access to other users for

User1 can **[answer choice]** the resource group.

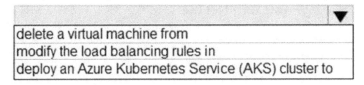

delete a virtual machine from
modify the load balancing rules in
deploy an Azure Kubernetes Service (AKS) cluster to

33) You have an Azure subscription named Subscription1 with a virtual network named VNet1 in a resource group named RG1. User1 in Subscription1 has the roles of Reader, Security Admin, and Security Reader. Your goal is to ensure that User1 can assign the Reader role for VNet1 to other users.

What action should you take?

A. Remove User1 from the Security Reader role for Subscription1. Assign User1 the Contributor role for RG1.

B. Assign User1 the Owner role for VNet1.

C. Assign User1 the Contributor role for VNet1.

D. Assign User1 the Network Contributor role for VNet1.

34) HOTSPOT –

You configure the custom role shown in the following exhibit.

```json
{
    "properties": {
        "roleName": "role1",
        "description": "",
        "roletype": "true",
        "assignableScopes": [
            "/subscriptions/3d6209d5-c714-4440-9556e-d6342086c2d7/"
        ],
        "permissions": [
            {
                "actions": [
                    "Microsoft.Authorization/*/read",
                    "Microsoft.Compute/availabilitySets/*",
                    "Microsoft.Compute/locations/*",
                    "Microsoft.Compute/virtualMachines/*",
                    "Microsoft.Compute/virtualMachineScaleSets/*",
                    "Microsoft.Compute/disks/write",
                    "Microsoft.Compute/disks/read",
                    "Microsoft.Compute/disks/delete",
                    "Microsoft.Network/locations/*",
                    "Microsoft.Network/networkInterfaces/*",
                    "Microsoft.Network/networkSecurityGroups/join/action",
                    "Microsoft.Network/networkSecurityGroups/read",
                    "Microsoft.Network/publicIPAddresses/join/action",
                    "Microsoft.Network/publicIPAddresses/read",
                    "Microsoft.Network/virtualNetworks/read",
                    "Microsoft.Network/virtualNetworks/subnets/join/action",
                    "Microsoft.Resources/deployments/*",
                    "Microsoft.Resources/subscriptions/resourceGroups/read",
                    "Microsoft.Support/*"
                ],
                "notActions": [],
                "dataActions": [],
                "notDataActions": []
            }
        ]
    }
}
```

Choose the answer choice that completes each statement based on the information presented in the graphic.

Hot Area:

Answer Area

To ensure that users can sign in to virtual machines that are assigned role1, modify the **[answer choice]** section

To ensure that role1 can be assigned only to a resource group named RG1, modify the **[answer choice]** section

35) You have an Azure subscription that contains a storage account named storage1. The storage1 account contains a file share named share1.

The subscription is linked to a hybrid Azure Active Directory (Azure AD) tenant that contains a security group named Group1.

You need to grant Group1 the Storage File Data SMB Share Elevated Contributor role for share1.

What should you do first?

A. Enable Active Directory Domain Service (AD DS) authentication for storage1.

B. Grant share-level permissions by using File Explorer.

C. Mount share1 by using File Explorer.

D. Create a private endpoint.

36) You have 15 Azure subscriptions.

You have an Azure Active Directory (Azure AD) tenant that contains a security group named Group1.

You plan to purchase additional Azure subscription.

You need to ensure that Group1 can manage role assignments for the existing subscriptions and the planned subscriptions. The solution must meet the following requirements:

☞ Use the principle of least privilege.

☞ Minimize administrative effort.

What should you do?

A. Assign Group1 the Owner role for the root management group.

B. Assign Group1 the User Access Administrator role for the root management group.

C. Create a new management group and assign Group1 the User Access Administrator role for the group.

D. Create a new management group and assign Group1 the Owner role for the group.

37) HOTSPOT –

You have an Azure subscription that contains the hierarchy shown in the following exhibit.

Tenant Root Group

ManagementGroup1

Subscription1

RG1

VM1

You create an Azure Policy definition named Policy1. To which Azure resources can you assign Policy1 and which Azure resources can you specify as exclusions from Policy1?

To answer, choose the appropriate options in the answer area.

Hot Area:

You can assign Policy1 to:

Subscription1 and RG1 only
ManagementGroup1 and Subscription1 only
Tenant Root Group, ManagementGroup1, and Subscription1 only
Tenant Root Group, ManagementGroup1, Subscription1, and RG1 only
Tenant Root Group, ManagementGroup1, Subscription1, RG1, and VM1

You can exclude Policy1 from:

VM1 only
RG1 and VM1 only
Subscription1, RG1, and VM1 only
ManagementGroup1, Subscription1, RG1, and VM1 only
Tenant Root Group, ManagementGroup1, Subscription1, RG1, and VM1

38) You have an Azure subscription that contains the following users in an Azure Active Directory tenant named contoso.onmicrosoft.com:

Name	Role	Scope
User1	Global administrator	Azure Active Directory
User2	Global administrator	Azure Active Directory
User3	User administrator	Azure Active Directory
User4	Owner	Azure Subscription

User1 creates a new Azure Active Directory tenant named external.contoso.onmicrosoft.com.

You need to create new user accounts in external.contoso.onmicrosoft.com.

Solution: You instruct User2 to create the user accounts.

Does that meet the goal?

A. Yes

B. No

39) You have an Azure subscription that contains the following users in an Azure Active Directory tenant named contoso.onmicrosoft.com:

Name	Role	Scope
User1	Global administrator	Azure Active Directory
User2	Global administrator	Azure Active Directory
User3	User administrator	Azure Active Directory
User4	Owner	Azure Subscription

User1 creates a new Azure Active Directory tenant named external.contoso.onmicrosoft.com.
You need to create new user accounts in external.contoso.onmicrosoft.com.
Solution: You instruct User4 to create the user accounts.

Does that meet the goal?

A. Yes

B. No

40) You have an Azure subscription that contains the following users in an Azure

Active   Directory   tenant   named
contoso.onmicrosoft.com:

Name	Role	Scope
User1	Global administrator	Azure Active Directory
User2	Global administrator	Azure Active Directory
User3	User administrator	Azure Active Directory
User4	Owner	Azure Subscription

User1 creates a new Azure Active Directory
tenant   named
external.contoso.onmicrosoft.com.
You need to create new user accounts in
external.contoso.onmicrosoft.com.
Solution: You instruct User3 to create the
user accounts.

Does that meet the goal?

A. Yes

B. No

41) You have two Azure subscriptions named Sub1 and Sub2.

An administrator creates a custom role that has an assignable scope to a resource group named RG1 in Sub1.

You need to ensure that you can apply the custom role to any resource group in Sub1 and Sub2. The solution must minimize administrative effort.

What should you do?

A. Select the custom role and add Sub1 and Sub2 to the assignable scopes. Remove RG1 from the assignable scopes.

B. Create a new custom role for Sub1. Create a new custom role for Sub2. Remove the role from RG1.

C. Create a new custom role for Sub1 and add Sub2 to the assignable scopes. Remove the role from RG1.

D. Select the custom role and add Sub1 to the assignable scopes. Remove RG1 from the assignable scopes. Create a new custom role for Sub2.

42) You have an Azure Subscription that contains a storage account named storageacct1234 and two users named User1 and User2.

You assign User1 the roles shown in the following exhibit.

User1 assignments – storageacct1234			✕

Assignments for the selected user, group, service principal, or managed identity at this scope or inherited to this scope.

🔍 Search by assignment name or description

Role assignments (2) ⓘ

Role	Scope	Group assignment	Condition
Reader	Resource group (inherited)	--	None
Storage Blob Data Contributor	This resource	--	Add

Deny assignments (0) ⓘ

Classic administrators (0) ⓘ

Which two actions can User1 perform?

Each correct answer presents a complete solution.

A. Assign roles to User2 for storageacct1234.

B. Upload blob data to storageacct1234.

C. Modify the firewall of storageacct1234.

D. View blob data in storageacct1234.

E. View file shares in storageacct1234.

43) You have an Azure subscription named Subscription1 that contains an Azure Log Analytics workspace named Workspace1.

You need to view the error events from a table named Event.

Which query should you run in Workspace1?

A. select * from Event where EventType == "error"

B. Event | search "error"

C. Event | where EventType is "error"

D. Get-Event Event | where {$_.EventType == "error"}

44) You have an Azure App Services web app named App1.

You plan to deploy App1 by using Web Deploy.

You need to ensure that the developers of App1 can use their Azure AD credentials to deploy content to App1. The solution must use the principle of least privilege.

What should you do?

A. Assign the Owner role to the developers

B. Configure app-level credentials for FTPS

C. Assign the Website Contributor role to the developers

D. Configure user-level credentials for FTPS

45) You have an Azure Active Directory (Azure AD) tenant named contoso.com.

You have a CSV file that contains the names and email addresses of 500 external users.

You need to create a guest user account in contoso.com for each of the 500 external users.

Solution: From Azure AD in the Azure portal, you use the Bulk invite user's operation.

Does this meet the goal?

A. Yes

B. No

46) HOTSPOT

You have an Azure subscription that is linked to an Azure AD tenant. The tenant contains the custom role-based access control (RBAC) roles shown in the following table.

Name	Description
Role1	Azure subscription role
Role2	Azure AD role

From the Azure portal, you need to create two custom roles named Role3 and Role4. Role3 will be an Azure subscription role. Role4 will be an Azure AD role.

Which roles can you clone to create the new roles?

Answer Area

Role3:

Role1 only
Built-in Azure subscription roles only
Role1 and built-in Azure subscription roles only
Built-in Azure subscription roles and built-in Azure AD roles only
Role1, Role2, built-in Azure subscription roles, and built-in Azure AD roles

Role4:

Role2 only
Built-in Azure AD roles only
Role2 and built-in Azure AD roles only
Built-in Azure AD roles and built-in Azure subscription roles only
Role1, Role2, built-in Azure AD, and built-in Azure subscription roles

47) DRAG DROP

You have an Azure subscription named Sub1 that contains two users named User1 and User2.

You need to assign role-based access control (RBAC) roles to User1 and User2. The users must be able to perform the following tasks in Sub1:

• User1 must view the data in any storage account.

• User2 must assign users the Contributor role for storage accounts.

The solution must use the principle of least privilege.

Which RBAC role should you assign to each user?

To answer, choose the appropriate roles to the correct users. Each role may be used once, more than once, or not at all.

BBAC roies:

a) Owner

b) Contributor

c) Reader and Data Access

d) Storage Account Contributor

Answer area:

User1:…………………………………………………………

User2:…………………………………………………………

48) You have an Azure subscription that contains 10 virtual machines, a key vault named Vault1, and a network security group (NSG) named NSG1. All the resources are deployed to the East US Azure region.

The virtual machines are protected by using NSG1. NSG1 is configured to block all outbound traffic to the internet.

You need to ensure that the virtual machines can access Vault1. The solution must use the principle of least privilege and minimize administrative effort

What should you configure as the destination of the outbound security rule for NSG1?

A. an application security group

B. a service tag

C. an IP address range

49) You have an Azure AD tenant named adatum.com that contains the groups shown in the following table.

Name	Member of
Group1	None
Group2	Group1
Group3	Group2

Adatum.com contains the users shown in the following table.

Name	Member of
User1	Group1
User2	Group2
User3	Group3
User4	None

You assign the Azure Active Directory Premium Plan 2 license to Group1 and User4.

Which users are assigned the Azure Active Directory Premium Plan 2 license?

A. User4 only

B. User1 and User4 only

C. User1, User2, and User4 only

D. User1, User2, User3, and User4

50) HOTSPOT

You have an Azure AD tenant named contoso.com.

You have two external partner organizations named fabrikam.com and litwareinc.com. Fabrikam.com is configured as a connected organization.

You create an access package as shown in the Access package exhibit. (Click the Access package tab.)

New access package   ...

* Basics   Resource roles   * Requests   Requestor information   * Lifecycle   **Review + Create**

Summary of access package configuration

Basics

Name	package1
Description	Guest users
Catalog name	General

Resource roles

Resource	Type	Sub Type	Role
Group1	Group and Team	Security Group	Member

Requests

Users who can request access	All configured connected organizations
Require approval	No
Enabled	Yes

Requestor information

Questions

Question	Answer format	Multiple choice optio...	Required

Attributes (Preview)

Attribute type	Attribute	Default display string	Answer format	Multi

Lifecycle

Access package assignments expire   After 365 days
Require access reviews   No

You configure the external user lifecycle settings as shown in the Lifecycle exhibit. (Click the Lifecycle tab.)

Manage the lifecycle of external users
Select what happens when an external user, who was added to your directory through an access package request, loses their last assignment to any access package.

Block external user from signing   [**Yes** | No]
in to this directory

Remove external user   [**Yes** | No]

Number of days before removing   [30]
external user from this directory

Delegate entitlement management
By default, only Global Administrators and User Administrators can create and manage catalogs, and can manage all catalogs. Users added to entitlement management as Catalog creators can also create catalogs and will become the owner of any catalogs they create.

Catalog creators ⓘ   0 selected

Add catalog creators

For each of the following statements, choose Yes if the statement is true. Otherwise, select No.

Statements:

1) Litwareinc.com users can be assigned to package1.

2) After 365 days, fabrikam.com users will be removed from Group1.

3) After 395 days, fabrikam.com users will be removed from contoso.com tenant.

51) You have an Azure subscription named Subscription1 that contains a virtual network named VNet1. VNet1 is in a resource group named RG1.

Subscription1 has a user named User1. User1 has the following roles:

• Reader

• Security Admin

• Security Reader

You need to ensure that User1 can assign the Reader role for VNet1 to other users.

What should you do?

A. Assign User1 the Network Contributor role for VNet1.

B. Remove User1 from the Security Reader role for Subscription1. Assign User1 the Contributor role for RG1.

C. Assign User1 the Owner role for VNet1.

D. Assign User1 the Network Contributor role for RG1.

52) HOTSPOT

You have an Azure subscription that contains the users shown in the following table.

Name	Member of
User1	Group1
User2	Group2
User3	Group3

The groups are configured as shown in the following table.

Name	Type	Azure AD roles can be assigned to the group
Group1	Security	Yes
Group2	Security	Yes
Group3	Microsoft 365	Yes

You have a resource group named RG1 as shown in the following exhibit.

RG1 | Access control (IAM)
Resource group

🔍 Search (Ctrl+/) « ╋ Add ↓ Download role assignments ≣≣ Edit columns ↻ Refresh ✕ Remo

| ⊞ Overview | Check access | Role assignments | Roles | Deny assignments | Classic administ |

Activity log

Access control (IAM) **Number of role assignments for this subscription** ⓘ

Tags

Resource visualizer 2 2000

Events

Settings 🔍 Search by name or email   Type : All   Role : All   Scope : All sc

Deployments 2 items (1 Users, 1 Groups)

Security

Policies

	Name	Type	Role	Scope	Condition
∨ Owner					
☐ GR	Group1	Group	Owner ⓘ	This resource	None
☐ PR	prvi prvi...	User	Owner ⓘ	Subscription (Inherited)	None

Properties

Locks

Answer area:

Statements:

1) You can assign User2 the owner role for RG1 by adding Group2 as a member of Group1.

2) You can assign User3 the owner role for RG1 by adding Group3 as a member of Group1.

3) You can assign User3 the owner role for RG1 by assigning the owner role to Group3 for.

53) You have an Azure subscription that contains the resources shown in the following table.

Name	Description
RG1	Resource group
RG2	Resource group
storage1	Storage account in RG1
Workspace1	Azure Synapse Analytics workspace in RG2

You need to assign Workspace1 a role to allow read, write, and delete operations for the data stored in the containers of storage1.

Which role should you assign?

A. Storage Account Contributor

B. Contributor

C. Storage Blob Data Contributor

D. Reader and Data Access

54) Your on-premises network contains a VPN gateway.

You have an Azure subscription that contains the resources shown in the following table.

Name	Type	Description
vgw1	Virtual network gateway	Gateway for Site-to-Site VPN to the on-premises network
storage1	Storage account	Standard performance tier
Vnet1	Virtual network	Enabled forced tunneling
VM1	Virtual machine	Connected to Vnet1

You need to ensure that all the traffic from VM1 to storage1 travels across the Microsoft backbone network.

What should you configure?

A. Azure Application Gateway

B. private endpoints

C. a network security group (NSG)

D. Azure Virtual WAN

55) HOTSPOT

You have an Azure subscription that

contains a user named User1 and the resources shown in the following table.

Name	Type
RG1	Resource group
networkinterface1	Virtual network interface
NSG1	Network security group (NSG)

NSG1 is associated to networkinterface1.

User1 has role assignments for NSG1 as shown in the following table.

Role	Scope
Contributor	This resource
Reader	Subscription (Inherited)
Storage Account Contributor	Resource group (Inherited)

For each of the following statements, choose Yes if the statement is true. Otherwise, select No.

Answer area:

Statements:

1) User1 can create a storage account in RG1.

2) User1 can modify the DNS settings of networkinterface1.

3) User1 can create an inbound security rule to filter inbound traffic to networkinterface1.

56) You have an Azure subscription named Subscription1 that contains a virtual network named VNet1. VNet1 is in a resource group named RG1.

Subscription1 has a user named User1. User1 has the following roles:

• Reader

• Security Admin

• Security Reader

You need to ensure that User1 can assign the Reader role for VNet1 to other users.

What should you do?

A. Remove User1 from the Security Reader role for Subscription1. Assign User1 the Contributor role for RG1.

B. Assign User1 the Access Administrator role for VNet1.

C. Remove User1 from the Security Reader and Reader roles for Subscription1. Assign User1 the Contributor role for Subscription1.

D. Assign User1 the Network Contributor role for RG1.

57) HOTSPOT

You have three Azure subscriptions named Sub1, Sub2, and Sub3 that are linked to an Azure AD tenant.

The tenant contains a user named User1, a security group named Group1, and a management group named MG1. User is a member of Group1.

Sub1 and Sub2 are members of MG1. Sub1 contains a resource group named RG1. RG1 contains five Azure functions.

You create the following role assignments for MG1:

- Group1: Reader
- User1: User Access Administrator

You assign User the Virtual Machine Contributor role for Sub1 and Sub2.

Answer area:

Statements:

1) The Group1 members can view the configurations of the Azure functions.

2) User1 can assign the owner role for RG1.

3) User1 can create a new resource group and deploy a virtual machine to the new group.

58) You have an Azure subscription that contains the resources shown in the following table.

Name	Description
share1	File share in storage1
storage1	Storage account
User1	Azure AD user

You need to assign User1 the Storage File Data SMB Share Contributor role for share1.

What should you do first?

A. Enable identity-based data access for the file shares in storage1.

B. Modify the security profile for the file shares in storage1.

C. Select Default to Azure Active Directory authorization in the Azure portal for storage1.

D. Configure Access control (IAM) for share1.

59) You have an Azure Active Directory (Azure AD) tenant named contoso.com.

You have a CSV file that contains the names and email addresses of 500 external users.

You need to create a guest user account in contoso.com for each of the 500 external users.

Solution: You create a PowerShell script that runs the New-MgInvitation cmdlet for each external user.

Does this meet the goal?

A. Yes

B. No

60) HOTSPOT

You have an Azure AD tenant named adatum.com that contains the groups shown in the following table.

Name	Type	Member of
Group1	Security	None
Group2	Security	Group1

Adatum.com contains the users shown in the following table.

Name	Member of
User1	Group1
User2	Group2

You assign an Azure Active Directory Premium P2 license to Group1 as shown in the   following   exhibit.

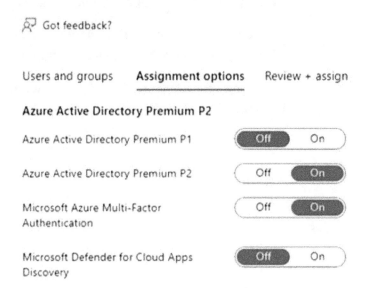

Group2 is NOT directly assigned a license.

For each of the following statements, choose Yes if the statement is true. Otherwise, select No.

Answer area:

Statements:

1) You can assign User1 the Microsoft Defender for Cloud Apps Discovery license.

2) You can remove the Azure Active Directory Premium P2 license from User1.

3) user2 is assigned the Azure Active Directory Premium P2.

Answers and Explanation

1) Correct Answer:

Box 1: Assign a tag to each resource

Box 2: From the Cost analysis blade, filter the view by tag

Box 3: Download the usage report

Box 1: Assign a tag to each resource.

You apply tags to your Azure resources giving metadata to logically organize them into a taxonomy. After you apply tags, you can retrieve all the resources in your subscription with that tag name and value. Each resource or resource group can have a maximum of 15 tag name/value pairs. Tags applied to the resource group are not inherited by the resources in that resource group.

Box 2: From the Cost analysis blade, filter the view by tag

After you get your services running, regularly check how much they're costing you. You can see the current spend and burn rate in Azure portal.

1. Visit the Subscriptions blade in Azure portal and select a subscription.

You should see the cost breakdown and burn rate in the popup blade.

2. Click Cost analysis in the list to the left to see the cost breakdown by resource. Wait 24 hours after you add a service for the data to populate.

3. You can filter by different properties like tags, resource group, and timespan. Click Apply to confirm the filters and download if you want to export the view to a

Comma-Separated Values (.csv) file.

Box 3: Download the usage report

Reference:

https://docs.microsoft.com/en-us/azure/azure-resource-manager/resource-group-using-tags
https://docs.microsoft.com/en-us/azure/billing/billing-getting-started

2) Correct answer: B

The correct query to run in Workspace1 to view the error events from a table named Event is:

B. search in (Event) "error"

This query will search for the term "error" in the Event table. The other options are not valid queries for Azure Log Analytics. Azure Log Analytics uses a version of the Kusto query language, and these queries do not conform to the correct syntax. For example, the 'select' statement is not used in Kusto, and PowerShell-style syntax (like option A) is not applicable here. Option D is incorrect because it attempts to use a mix of Kusto and PowerShell syntax.

Tested in lab Home>>Monitor>>Logs

All command queries return syntax error except Search in (Event) "error"

Reference:

https://docs.microsoft.com/en-us/azure/azure-monitor/log-query/search-queries

https://docs.microsoft.com/en-
us/azure/azure-monitor/log-query/get-
started-portal

https://docs.microsoft.com/en-
us/azure/data-
explorer/kusto/query/searchoperator?pivot
s=azuredataexplorer

3) Box 1: Yes

VNET1 is in the same region as VM1 and
VM2, so it can connect with both.

Box 2: Yes

Because both VMs are in different
Availability Zone, hence either one would
be available if one Data Center fails.

Box 3: No

If the Region fails then both VMs, which are
present in the Region will not be available.

Reference:

https://docs.microsoft.com/en-us/azure/architecture/resiliency/recovery-loss-azure-region

4) Correct Answer: A

You can only move a resource to a Resource Group or Subscription, but the location stays the same. When you move WebApp1 to RG2, the resource will be restricted based on the policy of the new Resource Group (Policy2).

You can move an app to another App Service plan, as long as the source plan and the target plan are in the same resource group and geographical region.

The region in which your app runs is the region of the App Service plan it's in. However, you cannot change an App Service plan's region.

Reference:

https://docs.microsoft.com/en-us/azure/app-service/app-service-plan-manage

5) 1) c, 2) a

"/subscriptions/c276fc76-9cd4-44c9-99a7-4fd71546435e"

"Microsoft.Authorization/"

Reference:

https://docs.microsoft.com/en-us/azure/role-based-access-control/custom-roles
https://docs.microsoft.com/en-us/azure/role-based-access-control/resource-provider-operations#microsoftresources

6) Correct Answer: AE

A: The customer sites are connected through VPNs, so an internal load balancer is enough.

B: The customer sites are connected through VPNs, so there's no need for a public load balancer, an internal load balancer is enough.

C: A CDN does not provide load balancing for applications, so it not relevant for this situation.

D: Traffic manager is a DNS based solution to direct users' requests to the nearest (typically) instance and does not provide load balancing for this situation.

E: Azure Application Gateway is a valid option, as it provides load balancing in addition to routing and security functions.

Network traffic from the VPN gateway is routed to the cloud application through an internal load balancer. The load balancer is located in the front-end subnet of the application.

Reference:

https://docs.microsoft.com/en-us/azure/architecture/reference-architectures/hybrid-networking/vpn

https://docs.microsoft.com/en-us/azure/load-balancer/load-balancer-overview

https://docs.microsoft.com/en-us/azure/application-gateway/overview

7) Correct Answer: B

Advisor helps you optimize and reduce your overall Azure spend by identifying idle and underutilized resources. You can get cost recommendations from the Cost tab on the Advisor dashboard.

Azure Advisor is a service in the Azure portal that provides personalized best practices and recommendations based on your usage and configurations. It helps you optimize your resources for high availability, security, performance, and cost. In this case, Advisor can provide recommendations for resizing or changing the service tier of virtual machines to save costs.

Reference:

https://docs.microsoft.com/en-us/azure/advisor/advisor-cost-recommendations

8) Correct answer:

- Select Users & Groups: Where you have to choose all users.

- Select Cloud apps or actions: to specify the Azure portal

- Grant: to grant the MFA.

Those are the minimum requirements to create MFA policy. No conditions are required in the question.

Reference:

https://docs.microsoft.com/en-us/azure/active-directory/conditional-access/concept-conditional-access-policies

9) Correct answer: A

To ensure that Admin1 can invite the external partner to sign in to the Azure AD tenant, you should:

A. From the Users settings blade, modify the External collaboration settings.

Explanation:

The "External collaboration settings" in the Users settings blade allow you to control external user access to your organization's data and resources. By modifying these settings, you can enable or disable external collaboration and manage how users from other organizations can access your Azure AD tenant.

Option B (Custom domain names) is not directly related to external collaboration settings. It's more about adding custom domains to your Azure AD.

Option C (Organizational relationships) is used for configuring partnerships between organizations, but it's not the primary setting for inviting external users.

Option D (Roles and administrators' blade) is not necessary for inviting external users; the User administrator role should be sufficient for this scenario.

Therefore, the correct answer is A. From the Users settings blade, modify the External collaboration settings.

Go to Azure AD--users--user settings --scroll down. --External users

Manage external collaboration settings.

You can adjust the guest user settings, their access, who can invite them from "External collaboration settings"

Reference:

https://docs.microsoft.com/en-us/azure/active-directory/external-identities/delegate-invitations

10) Correct answer: C

No one is given default access to the root management group. Azure AD Global Administrators are the only users that can elevate themselves to gain access. Once they have access to the root management group, the global administrators can assign any Azure role to other users to manage it.

Reference:

https://docs.microsoft.com/en-us/azure/governance/management-groups/overview#important-facts-about-the-root-management-group

https://docs.microsoft.com/en-us/azure/governance/management-groups/overview

11) 1) a, 2) d

Box 1: Group 1 only -

First rule applies -

Box 2: Group1 and Group2 only -

Both membership rules apply.

Reference:

https://docs.microsoft.com/en-
us/sccm/core/clients/manage/collections/c
reate-collections

12) Correct Answer: 1) c, 2) d

Box 1: User1 and User3 only

You must use Windows Server Active
Directory to update the identity, contact
info, or job info for users whose source of
authority is Windows Server Active
Directory.

Box 2: User1, User2, and User3

Usage location is an Azure property that can only be modified from Azure AD (for all users including Windows Server AD users synced via Azure AD Connect).

Reference:

https://docs.microsoft.com/en-us/azure/active-directory/fundamentals/active-directory-users-profile-azure-portal

13) Correct Answer: A - Yes

Your account must have any one of the following Azure roles at the subscription scope: Owner, Contributor, Reader, or Network Contributor.

Network Contributor role - Lets you manage networks, but not access to them.

Traffic Analytics is a cloud-based solution that provides visibility into user and application activity in cloud networks. Traffic analytics analyzes Network Watcher network security group (NSG) flow logs to provide insights into traffic flow in your Azure cloud.

Reference:

https://docs.microsoft.com/en-us/azure/network-watcher/traffic-analytics

https://docs.microsoft.com/en-us/azure/network-watcher/traffic-analytics-faq

https://docs.microsoft.com/en-us/azure/network-watcher/traffic-analytics#user-access-requirements

https://docs.microsoft.com/en-us/azure/role-based-access-control/built-in-roles

14) Correct Answer: A

Your account must have any one of the following Azure roles at the subscription scope: Owner, Contributor, Reader, or Network Contributor.

Network Contributor role - Lets you manage networks, but not access to them.

Traffic Analytics is a cloud-based solution that provides visibility into user and application activity in cloud networks. Traffic analytics analyzes Network Watcher network security group (NSG) flow logs to provide insights into traffic flow in your Azure cloud.

Reference:

https://docs.microsoft.com/en-us/azure/network-watcher/traffic-analytics

https://docs.microsoft.com/en-us/azure/network-watcher/traffic-analytics-faq

https://docs.microsoft.com/en-us/azure/network-watcher/traffic-analytics#user-access-requirements

https://docs.microsoft.com/en-us/azure/role-based-access-control/built-in-roles

15) Correct Answer: A - Yes

Your account must have any one of the following Azure roles at the subscription scope: owner, contributor, reader, or network contributor.

Reader role - View all resources, but does not allow you to make any changes.

Traffic Analytics is a cloud-based solution that provides visibility into user and application activity in cloud networks. Traffic analytics analyzes Network Watcher network security group (NSG) flow logs to provide insights into traffic flow in your Azure cloud.

Reference:

https://docs.microsoft.com/en-us/azure/network-watcher/traffic-analytics

https://docs.microsoft.com/en-us/azure/network-watcher/traffic-analytics-faq

https://docs.microsoft.com/en-us/azure/network-watcher/traffic-analytics#user-access-requirements

https://docs.microsoft.com/en-us/azure/role-based-access-control/built-in-roles

16) Correct Answer: C

Only Owner and Contributor can perform the actions, but we need to follow the least privilege principal, so Contributor.

A: Owner- Grants full access to manage all resources, including the ability to assign roles in Azure RBAC.

B: Virtual Machine Contributor - Create and manage virtual machines, manage disks and disk snapshots, install and run software, reset password of the root user of the virtual machine using VM extensions, and manage local user accounts using VM extensions. This role does not grant you management access to the virtual network or storage account the virtual machines are connected to. This role does not allow you to assign roles in Azure RBAC.

C: Contributor - Grants full access to manage all resources, but does not allow you to assign roles in Azure RBAC, manage assignments in Azure Blueprints, or share image galleries.

D: Virtual Machine Administrator Login - View Virtual Machines in the portal and login as administrator.

Reference:

https://docs.microsoft.com/en-us/azure/role-based-access-control/built-in-roles

17) Correct Answer:

Azure (RBAC) and Azure AD roles are independent. AD roles do not grant access to resources and Azure roles do not grant access to Azure AD. However, a Global Administrator in AD can elevate access to all subscriptions and will be User Access Administrator in Azure root scope.

All 3 users are GA (AD) and Admin3 is owner of the subscription (RBAC).

Admin1 has elevated access, so he is also User Access Admin (RBAC).

To assign a user the owner role at the Subscription scope, you require permissions, such as User Access Admin or Owner.

Box 1: Yes

Admin1 has elevated access, so he is User Access Admin. This is valid.

Box 2: Yes

Admi3 is Owner of the Subscription. This is valid.

Box 3: No

Admin2 is just a GA in Azure AD scope. He doesn't have permission in the Subscription.

Reference:

https://docs.microsoft.com/en-us/azure/role-based-access-control/elevate-access-global-admin

https://docs.microsoft.com/en-us/azure/role-based-access-control/role-assignments-portal-subscription-admin

18) Correct Answer: A

Managed identities for Azure resources provide Azure services with an automatically managed identity in Azure Active Directory. You can use this identity to authenticate to any service that supports Azure AD authentication, without having credentials in your code. You can enable and disable the system-assigned managed identity for VM using the Azure portal.

RBAC manages who has access to Azure resources, what areas they have access to and what they can do with those resources. Examples of Role Based Access Control (RBAC) include: Allowing an app to access all resources in a resource group Policies on the other hand focus on resource properties during deployment and for already existing resources. As an example, a policy can be issued to ensure users can only deploy DS series VMs within a specified resource

Reference:

https://docs.microsoft.com/en-us/azure/active-directory/managed-identities-azure-resources/qs-configure-portal-windows-vm

19) Correct Answer: B

When you delete a resource group, all of its resources are also deleted. Deleting a resource group deletes all of its template deployments and currently stored operations.

As an administrator, you can lock a subscription, resource group, or resource to prevent other users in your organization from accidentally deleting or modifying critical resources. The lock overrides any permissions the user might have.

You can't delete a vault that contains backup data. Once backup data is deleted, it will go into the soft deleted state.

So, you have to remove the lock on order to delete the VNET and delete the backups in order to delete the vault.

Reference:

https://docs.microsoft.com/en-us/azure/azure-resource-manager/management/delete-resource-group?tabs=azure-powershell

https://docs.microsoft.com/en-us/azure/azure-resource-manager/management/lock-resources

https://docs.microsoft.com/en-us/azure/backup/backup-azure-delete-vault#before-you-start

20) Correct Answer: A

An NS record or (name server record) tells recursive name servers which name servers are authoritative for a zone. You can have as many NS records as you would like in your zone file. The benefit of having multiple NS records is the redundancy of your DNS service.

You need to create a name server (NS) record for the zone.

The NS (Name Server) record is used to delegate a subdomain to a different set of authoritative DNS servers. To delegate the subdomain research.adatum.com, you should create an NS record named "research" in the adatum.com zone and specify the DNS servers responsible for handling the research.adatum.com subdomain.

Options B, C, and D are not relevant for delegating a subdomain to a different DNS server:

B. Creating a PTR record is used for reverse DNS lookups, not for delegation.

C. Modifying the SOA (Start of Authority) record is not the correct step for delegating a subdomain.

D. Creating an A record for *.research is not about delegation; it's about defining a wildcard entry for the A (IPv4 address) record in the zone.

Therefore, the correct answer is A. Create an NS record named research in the adatum.com zone.

Reference:

https://docs.microsoft.com/en-us/azure/dns/delegate-subdomain

21)

Here are the steps we need to perform in sequence:

1) Add a custom name: add a custom domain name to Azure AD from the

"Custom domain names" page in the Azure portal. When we add a custom domain name, Azure AD gives us the information we need to create DNS records at the domain name registrar.

2) Add a record to the public contoso.com DNS zone: we need to add a DNS record at our domain name registrar to verify that we own the domain. This record is typically a TXT or MX record for domain verification.

3) Verify the domain: After we've added the DNS record at the domain name registrar, then we can go back to the Azure portal to verify the domain. Azure AD checks if the DNS record exists and if it does, the domain is verified.

Reference:

https://docs.microsoft.com/en-us/azure/dns/dns-web-sites-custom-domain

22) Correct answer: B

To view the error events from a table named Event in an Azure Log Analytics workspace named Workspace1, you should run the following query:

B. Kusto Query Language (KQL) to search for error events:

search in (Event) "error"

So, the correct answer is B. search in (Event) "error".

Reference:

https://docs.microsoft.com/en-us/azure/azure-monitor/logs/log-analytics-tutorial

23) Correct answer: D

Registrar "owns" the Top-level Domain and will have their NS registered against the domain by default. By changing the registrar NS records to point to your Azure DNS NS records you take ownership into your Azure DNS.

To ensure that records created in the contoso.com zone are resolvable from the internet, you need to modify the NS (Name Server) records in the DNS domain registrar.

When you create a public Azure DNS zone named contoso.com, Azure assigns a set of NS records for that zone. These NS records specify the name servers responsible for handling DNS queries for the contoso.com domain. To make the records in the Azure DNS zone resolvable from the internet, you need to update the NS records at the DNS domain registrar to point to the name servers provided by Azure.

Reference:

https://docs.microsoft.com/en-us/azure/dns/dns-delegate-domain-azure-dns

24)

1) You can assign the Storage File Data SMB Share Contributor role to User1 for Share1 = "YES"

2) You can assign the Storage File Data SMB Share Reader role to Computer1 for Share1 = "NO"

3) You can assign the Storage File Data SMB Share Elevated Contributor role to User2 for Share1 = "YES"

"Azure AD DS and on-premises AD DS authentication don't support authentication against computer accounts."

Reference:

https://docs.microsoft.com/en-us/azure/storage/files/storage-files-active-directory-overview#restrictions

25)

1) Add a subnet to VNET1 = "User1 and User3 only"

2) Assign a user the Reader role to VNEt1 = "User1 only"

Explanation:

User1 - The Owner Role lets you manage everything, including access to resources.

User3 - The Network Contributor role lets you manage networks, including creating subnets.

User2 - The Security Admin role can view security policies, view security states, edit security policies, view alerts and recommendations, dismiss alerts and recommendations.

Security admin can't add subnets.

Only owner can assign roles.

Reference:

https://docs.microsoft.com/en-us/azure/role-based-access-control/built-in-roles https://docs.microsoft.com/en-us/azure/role-based-access-control/resource-provider-operations#microsoftnetwork

26)

Box 1: Sub1, RG1, and VM1 only -

You can lock a subscription, resource group, or resource to prevent other users in your organization from accidentally deleting or modifying critical resources.

Box 2: Sub1, RG1, and VM1 only -

You apply tags to your Azure resources, resource groups, and subscriptions.

Only can assign locks and tags to subscriptions, resource groups and resources. Tested in lab

Both Tags and Locks are available to Subscriptions, Resource Groups, and Resources.

See FIRST Paragraph in both References:

Ref Locks:

https://docs.microsoft.com/en-us/azure/azure-resource-manager/management/lock-resources?tabs=json

Ref Tags:

https://docs.microsoft.com/en-us/azure/azure-resource-manager/management/tag-resources?tabs=json

27) Correct answer: B

To perform a bulk, delete of users in Azure Active Directory, you need to create and upload a CSV file that contains the list of users to be deleted. The file should include the user's principal name (UPN) of each user only. Therefore, the answer is B. The user's principal name of each user only.

When you use the bulk delete feature in the Azure Active Directory admin center, you need to specify the UPN for each user that you want to delete. The UPN is a unique identifier for each user in Azure AD and is the primary way that Azure AD identifies and manages user accounts.

Including additional attributes like the display name or usage location is not required for the bulk delete operation, as the UPN is the only mandatory attribute for the user account. However, you may include additional attributes in the CSV file if you want to keep track of the metadata associated with each user account.

Reference:

https://docs.microsoft.com/en-us/azure/active-directory/enterprise-users/users-bulk-delete

28)

1) No: Azure policy was created before the RG1 was assigned tag, which means when RG1 was manually assigned tag Tag2:IT, the policy will take action to append

Tag4:value4 to RG1. Note that policy action is to "append", that means whatever else tag RG1 is given won't be taken away. As such RG1 will have two tags, Tag2:IT and Tag4:value4

2) No: Remember tags are not inheritable, whatever tag assigned to RG1 won't be applied to any resources under it. As such the Storage1 should be Tag3:value1 and Tag4:value4.

3) No: vNet1 is excluded from the Azure policy, hence the policy won't do anything to it. As such vNet1 should only have the tag manually assigned: Tag3:value2. PS, I take that "Exclusions: Sub1/RG1/VNET1" does not mean both RG1 & vNet1 are excluded, only vNet1 is excluded, the Sub1/RG1/VNET1 is merely a path to the object that is excluded.

Reference:

https://docs.microsoft.com/en-us/azure/azure-resource-

manager/management/tag-
resources?tabs=json

29) Correct answer: B

No, assigning the Traffic Manager
Contributor role to Admin1 at the
subscription level will not meet the goal of
enabling Traffic Analytics for the Azure
subscription.

The Traffic Manager Contributor role only
grants permissions to manage Traffic
Manager profiles, endpoints, and traffic
routing methods, but it does not provide
the necessary permissions to enable Traffic
Analytics for the Azure subscription.

To enable Traffic Analytics for an Azure
subscription, you need to assign the Log
Analytics Contributor role to the Azure AD
user named Admin1. The Log Analytics
Contributor role allows the user to manage
Log Analytics workspaces, which is required
to enable Traffic Analytics for the Azure
subscription.

Therefore, assigning the Traffic Manager Contributor role to Admin1 will not meet the goal of enabling Traffic Analytics for the Azure subscription.

Reference:

https://docs.microsoft.com/en-us/azure/network-watcher/traffic-analytics-faq

30) Correct answer: B

Administrative units restrict permissions in a role to any portion of your organization that you define. You could, for example, use administrative units to delegate the Helpdesk Administrator role to regional support specialists, so they can manage users only in the region that they support.

"It can be useful to restrict administrative scope by using administrative units in organizations that are made up of independent divisions of any kind.

Reference:

https://docs.microsoft.com/en-us/azure/active-directory/roles/administrative-units#deployment-scenario

31) Correct answer: A

Logic App Contributor role will allow you to create Logic Apps.

"Your Azure subscription requires Contributor permissions for the resource group that contains that logic app resource. If you create a logic app resource, you automatically have Contributor access."

Reference:

https://docs.microsoft.com/en-us/azure/logic-apps/logic-apps-securing-a-logic-app?tabs=azure-portal

32)

1) User1 can "assign access to other users for" LB1.

2) User1 can "delete a virtual machine from" the resource group.

The Role assignments say it all.

Create and manage virtual machines, manage disks, install and run software, reset password of the root user of the virtual machine using VM extensions, and manage local user accounts using VM extensions. This role does not grant you management access to the virtual network or storage account the virtual machines are connected to. This role does not allow you to assign roles in Azure RBAC.

Reference:

https://docs.microsoft.com/en-us/azure/role-based-access-control/built-in-roles#virtual-machine-contributor https://docs.microsoft.com/en-us/azure/role-based-access-control/rbac-and-directory-admin-roles

33) Correct answer: B

Owner = Grants full access to manage all resources, including the ability to assign roles in Azure RBAC.

Contributor = Grants full access to manage all resources, but does NOT allow you to assign roles in Azure RBAC. (you cannot add users or changes their rights)

User Access Administrator = Lets you manage user access to Azure resources.

Reader = View all resources, but does not allow you to make any changes.

Security Admin = View and update permissions for Security Center. Same permissions as the Security Reader role and can also update the security policy and dismiss alerts and recommendations.

Network Contributor = Lets you manage networks, but not access to them. (so, you can add VNET, subnet, etc.)

Reference:

https://docs.microsoft.com/en-us/azure/role-based-access-control/rbac-and-directory-admin-roles

https://docs.microsoft.com/en-us/azure/role-based-access-control/overview

34) correct answer is dataActions and assignableScopes.

You need to provide either of the following in DataActions:

Microsoft.Compute/virtualMachines/login/action

Microsoft.Compute/virtualMachines/loginAsAdmin/action

Reference:

https://docs.microsoft.com/en-us/azure/role-based-access-control/built-in-roles?source=recommendations#virtual-machine-administrator-login

35) Correct answer: A

A. Enable Active Directory Domain Service (AD DS) authentication for storage1.

To grant the Group1 the Storage File Data SMB Share Elevated Contributor role for share1, you need to enable Active Directory Domain Service (AD DS) authentication for the storage account.

By enabling AD DS authentication, you allow Azure AD security groups to be used for granting access control to file shares in the storage account. This enables you to assign roles, such as the Storage File Data SMB Share Elevated Contributor role, to the security group Group1 for the specific file share share1.

Once AD DS authentication is enabled and the security group is assigned the appropriate role, Group1 will have the necessary permissions to access and manage the file share.

Therefore, enabling Active Directory Domain Service (AD DS) authentication for storage1 is the first step you should take to grant Group1 the Storage File Data SMB Share Elevated Contributor role for share1.

" Enable Active Directory Domain Service (AD DS) authentication for storage1. "

Reference:

https://docs.microsoft.com/en-us/azure/storage/files/storage-files-identity-auth-active-directory-domain-service-enable?tabs=azure-portal#overview-of-the-workflow

36) Correct answer: B

The User Access Administrator role enables the user to grant other users access to Azure resources. This switch can be helpful to regain access to a subscription.

Management groups give you enterprise-grade management at scale no matter what type of subscriptions you might have.

Each directory is given a single top-level management group called the "Root" management group. This root management group is built into the hierarchy to have all management groups and subscriptions fold up to it. This root management group allows for global policies and Azure role assignments to be applied at the directory level.

Incorrect:

Not C: A few directories that started using management groups early in the preview before June 25 2018 could see an issue where not all the subscriptions were within the hierarchy. The process to have all subscriptions in the hierarchy was put in place after a role or policy assignment was done on the root management group in the directory.

"Assign Group1 the User Access Administrator role for the root management group."

To be able to assign licenses to all current and future subscriptions, while minimizing the administrative effort, one should apply the role to the Root Management Group.

And because we should use the principle of least privilege, we should choose the User Access Administrator role instead of the Owner one.

Reference:

https://docs.microsoft.com/en-us/azure/role-based-access-control/rbac-and-directory-admin-roles

https://docs.microsoft.com/en-us/azure/governance/management-groups/overview

37) The correct answer is ""ManagementGroup1, Subscription1, RG1 only and VM1 only""

We've tested it at an Azure lab.

In the scope field at the "Basics" tab we were able to select "Tenant Root Group" or "Management Group1" with the optional entries of Subscription and Resource group

So ""you can assign policy to Tenant Root Group,ManagementGroup1,Subscription1 and RG1""

As for the second answer about the exclusions, we were able to select all the items in the scope EXCEPT the Tenant Root Group.

38) Correct answer: A

Only User1 has access to the new Tenant, because User1 created the Tenant and became automatically Global Admin.

User1 is global admin of contoso.onmicrosoft.com.

As he created the new tenant called external.contoso.onmicrosoft.com, he will be the OWNER. Check the scope not just the role.

Reference:

https://docs.microsoft.com/en-us/azure/devops/organizations/accounts/add-users-to-azure-ad

39) Correct answer: B

No, when you create a new tenant, the creator is the only global admin and owner, he must first give access to others to allow anything.

Even if User4 is owner of subscription, he was not able to find new tenant created by user1 in Azure Active Directory > Manage Tenant.

Reference:

https://docs.microsoft.com/en-us/azure/active-directory/fundamentals/active-directory-access-create-new-tenant#your-user-account-in-the-new-tenant

40) Correct answer: B

We've tested this.

1. We created a new Tenant contosogmpp.

2. Added 2 users, User1 and User 2 in this tenant and gave them global privileges

3. We logged through User1 and created a new tenant called externalcontossgmpp

4. Now when, we logged in through User2 and try to switch tenants, the new tenant externalcontossgmpp is not available at all for User2.

Hence User1 needs to invite User2 first.

Only a global administrator can add users to this tenant.

Reference:

https://docs.microsoft.com/en-us/azure/devops/organizations/accounts/add-users-to-azure-ad

41) Correct answer: A

A) " Select the custom role and add Sub1 and Sub2 to the assignable scopes. Remove RG1 from the assignable scopes. "

To assure the solution minimizes the administrative effort, we just need to change the assignable scope list of the custom role.

Reference:

https://docs.microsoft.com/en-us/azure/role-based-access-control/custom-roles#custom-role-properties

42) Correct answer: BD

Reader: View all resources, but does not allow you to make any changes. So User1 can "View blob data in storageacct1234"

Storage Blob Data Contributor: Allows for read, write and delete access to Azure Storage blob containers and data. So User1 can "Upload blob data to storageacct1234"

Tried this in the Lab

A. User1 cannot add role assignment (disabled)

B. Worked - User1 can upload blob data

C. Nope

D. Worked - User1 can view blob data

E. Error - The client 'user1@..... does not have authorization to perform action 'Microsoft.Storage/storageAccounts/listKeys/action' over scope '/subscriptions/...../resourceGroups/rg1/providers/Microsoft.Storage/storageAccounts/storage1234

Reference:

https://learn.microsoft.com/en-us/azure/role-based-access-control/built-in-roles#reader

View all resources, but does not allow you to make any changes.

https://learn.microsoft.com/en-us/azure/role-based-access-control/built-in-roles#storage-blob-data-contributor

Read, write, and delete Azure Storage containers and blobs.

43) Correct answer: B

Other correct answer option can come in the following form:

Search in (Event) "Error"

Event | where eventType = "Error"

44) Correct answer: C

C. Assign the Website Contributor role to the developers.

To allow the developers of App1 to use their Azure AD credentials to deploy content to App1 using Web Deploy, you should assign the Website Contributor role to the developers. This role provides the necessary permissions for developers to deploy content to the web app, but does not grant them excessive permissions that could be used to make unwanted changes.

Option A is not recommended as it would grant excessive permissions to the developers, which could be used to make unwanted changes.

Option B and D are not relevant to the scenario as the question is specifically asking for how to use Azure AD credentials for Web Deploy, not FTPS.

Option C is a potential solution, but the Website Contributor role provides a more targeted and appropriate level of permissions for the scenario.

45) Correct answer: B

The question states "You have a CSV file that contains the names and email addresses of 500 external users."

This implies that the required fields (Email and Redirection URL) are missing from the .csv file.

The Bulk invite user's operation in Azure AD is used for inviting multiple guest users to the organization, but it is not specifically designed for bulk creation of guest user accounts. The operation sends invitations to the external users, and they need to accept the invitations to become guest users in the Azure AD tenant.

If you want to directly create guest user accounts for the external users without sending invitations, you might need to use PowerShell or the Microsoft Graph API to perform bulk creation. The Bulk invite user's operation, as described, involves inviting users rather than creating user accounts directly.

Therefore, the provided solution does not meet the goal of creating guest user accounts directly for the 500 external users.

Here are the csv field pre-requisites that are needed for bulk upload of external users:

https://learn.microsoft.com/en-us/azure/active-directory/external-identities/tutorial-bulk-invite#prerequisites

46)

Role3: Role1 and built-in Azure subscription roles only

Role4: Role2 only

Explanation: You cannot clone built-in Azure AD role.

47)

Answer Area

User1: | Reader and Data Access |

User2: | Owner |

"Reader and Data Access":

"Lets you view everything but will not let you delete or create a storage account or contained resource. It will also allow read/write access to all data contained in a storage account via access to storage account keys."

"Owner" is needed to manage permissions, as "User Access Administrator" is not offered as an option.

48) The correct answer: B. a service tag.

In order to ensure that the virtual machines can access Vault1 while also using the principle of least privilege and minimizing administrative effort, you should configure a service tag as the destination of the outbound security rule for NSG1. Service tags represent a group of IP addresses associated with Azure PaaS and SaaS services. By specifying a service tag as the destination of the outbound security rule, you can allow the virtual machines to access Vault1 without having to manually specify the IP addresses of Vault1. This reduces administrative effort and ensures that the virtual machines are only able to access Vault1, rather than any other internet destination.

Reference:

https://learn.microsoft.com/en-us/azure/virtual-network/service-tags-overview#available-service-tags

"AzureKeyVault" tag can be used in outbound NSGs.

49) Correct answer: B

Under Limitations and known issues:

"Group-based licensing currently does not support groups that contain other groups (nested groups). If you apply a license to a nested group, only the immediate first-level user members of the group have the licenses applied."

"You assign the Azure Active Directory Premium Plan 2 license to Group1 and User4."

User 4 is assigned the license directly.

A. User4 only (INCORRECT = Also Group1 has directly assigned licenses)

B. User1 and User4 only (CORRECT = Both have directly assigned license)

C. User1, User2, and User4 only (INCORRECT = User2 is member of Group2 that is NESTED to Group1. NESTED Group are NOT Supported as per MS KB: Group-based licensing currently does not support groups that contain other groups (nested groups). If you apply a license to a nested group, only the immediate first-level user members of the group have the licenses applied.

D. User1, User2, User3, and User4 (INCORRECT= Same reason answer C)

Reference:

https://learn.microsoft.com/en-us/azure/active-directory/enterprise-users/licensing-group-advanced

50)

1) No - Because not Connected

2) Yes - Because when it expires it is removed from the group. Proof to follow

3) Yes - 365 + 30 = 395

When a user's access package assignment expires, they are removed from the group or team, unless they currently have an assignment to another access package that includes that same group or team.

Reference:

removedhttps://learn.microsoft.com/en-us/azure/active-directory/governance/entitlement-management-access-package-resources

51) Correct answer: C

There are only two choices for that purpose;

- Assign User1 the Owner role for VNet1.

- Assign User1 the User Access Administrator role for VNet1.

52)

1. No - Nesting is currently not supported for groups that can be assigned to a role.

2. No - M365 groups can't be added in security groups.

3. Yes - Yes, you can assign owner role for user 3 in RG1

Add or remove a group from another group

You can add an existing Security group to another Security group (also known as nested groups). Depending on the group types, you can add a group as a member of another group, just like a user, which applies settings like roles and access to the nested groups. You'll need the Groups Administrator or User Administrator role to edit group membership.

We currently don't support:

Adding groups to a group synced with on-premises Active Directory.

Adding Security groups to Microsoft 365 groups.

Adding Microsoft 365 groups to Security groups or other Microsoft 365 groups.

Assigning apps to nested groups.

Applying licenses to nested groups.

Adding distribution groups in nesting scenarios.

Adding security groups as members of mail-enabled security groups.

Adding groups as members of a role-assignable group.

Reference:

https://learn.microsoft.com/en-us/azure/active-directory/fundamentals/how-to-manage-groups

53) Correct answer: C

Storage Blob Data Contributor Read, write, and delete Azure Storage containers and blobs.

To allow Azure Synapse Analytics workspace (Workspace1) to perform read, write, and delete operations for the data stored in the containers of storage1, you should assign the "Storage Blob Data Contributor" role.

So, the correct answer is: C. Storage Blob Data Contributor

Option A, "Storage Account Contributor," grants permissions to manage the Azure Storage account itself, including its configuration and settings, but it doesn't provide the necessary permissions to perform read, write, and delete operations on the data stored within the containers of the storage account.

Reference:

https://learn.microsoft.com/en-
us/azure/role-based-access-control/built-in-
roles#storage-blob-data-contributor

54) Correct answer: B

Per the MS documentation, private
endpoint seems to be the proper choice:
"You can use private endpoints for your
Azure Storage accounts to allow clients on a
virtual network (VNet) to securely access
data over a Private Link. The private
endpoint uses a separate IP address from
the VNet address space for each storage
account service. Network traffic between
the clients on the VNet and the storage
account traverses over the VNet and a
private link on the Microsoft backbone
network, eliminating exposure from the
public internet."

Reference:

https://learn.microsoft.com/en-us/azure/storage/common/storage-private-endpoints

55) YES, No, Yes

1) (YES) User1 can create a storage account in RG1, since User1 has Storage Account Contribute Role inherited from Resource Group.

2) (NO) User1 can modify the DNS settings of networkinterface1, since it requires Network Contribute role referring to the following link.

https://learn.microsoft.com/en-us/azure/virtual-network/virtual-network-network-interface?tabs=network-interface-portal#permissions

3) (YES) User1 can create an inbound security rule to filter inbound traffic to networkinterface1, since User1 has Contributor role for NSG1

References:

https://learn.microsoft.com/en-us/azure/role-based-access-control/built-in-roles#storage-account-contributor

-Microsoft.Storage/storageAccounts/*
Create and manage storage accounts

https://learn.microsoft.com/en-us/azure/role-based-access-control/built-in-roles#reader

View all resources, but does not allow you to make any changes.

https://learn.microsoft.com/en-us/azure/role-based-access-control/built-in-roles#contributor

Grants full access to manage all resources, but does not allow you to assign roles in Azure RBAC, manage assignments in Azure Blueprints, or share image galleries.

56) Correct answer: B

You need to have the Owner Role or Access Administrator role to assign roles but

Access Administrator role is preferred as it is least privilege.

A: Removing Security Reader won't grant additional permissions for assigning roles. Contributor for RG1 only manages resources within the group, not role assignment.

C: Removing Reader and Security Reader is unnecessary and removes existing access. Additionally, Contributor for Subscription1 is too broad and grants too many privileges.

D: Network Contributor only manages network resources like subnets and load balancers, not role assignment for VNet1.

The Access Administrator role specifically grants the "Microsoft.Authorization/roleAssignments/write" permission, which allows adding and removing role assignments, including assigning the Reader role for VNet1 to other users. This role provides the exact capability required without granting excessive permissions.

Therefore, B. Assign User1 the Access Administrator role for VNet1 is the correct solution to enable User1 to assign the Reader role for VNet1 to other users.

Reference:

https://learn.microsoft.com/en-us/azure/role-based-access-control/rbac-and-directory-admin-roles

57)

1) Yes, GROUP1 Reader access, provides access to view all items, except secrets

https://learn.microsoft.com/en-us/azure/role-based-access-control/built-in-roles#reader

2) Yes, To Assign OWNER role, you need to either Owner role or User Administrator Access Role

https://learn.microsoft.com/en-us/azure/role-based-access-control/role-

assignments-portal-subscription-
admin#prerequisites

3) No, Neither User Access Admin Role nor the Reader Role allows to create new resources.

User1 cannot create a new resource group and deploy a virtual machine to the new group. While User1 has the User Access Administrator role at the management group level (MG1), this role does not grant the user permissions to create resource groups or deploy virtual machines directly. The User Access Administrator role allows User1 to manage access to Azure resources but does not provide the necessary permissions for resource creation or deployment.

To create a new resource group and deploy a virtual machine, User1 would need appropriate permissions at the subscription or resource group level, such as the Contributor role. In this scenario, User1 has been assigned the Virtual Machine Contributor role for Sub1 and Sub2, so they have the necessary permissions to work within those specific subscriptions but not at the management group or Azure AD tenant level.

https://learn.microsoft.com/en-us/azure/role-based-access-control/role-assignments-steps

58) Correct answer: A

We just created a storage account,

then created a file share,

went to IAM,

And it says: To give individual accounts access to the file share (Kerberos), enable identity-based authentication for the storage account.

The correct steps to assign User1 the Storage File Data SMB Share Contributor role for share1 are:

1. Enable identity-based data access for the file shares in storage1.

2. Configure Access control (IAM) for share1 and add User1 as a role assignment with the Storage File Data SMB Share Contributor role.

So, the correct answer is A.

59) Correct answer: A

The New-MgInvitation cmdlet is part of the Microsoft Graph PowerShell module. It's used to create an invitation to an external user. When the invited user redeems their invitation, a guest user is created in the directory.

If you use a PowerShell script that loops through each external user in the CSV file and runs the New-MgInvitation cmdlet for each of them, it will send out invitation emails to each of those external users. Once an external user accepts the invitation, they'll be added to the Azure AD tenant as a guest user.

So, using the New-MgInvitation cmdlet in a PowerShell script for each external user does meet the goal of creating a guest user account in contoso.com for each of the 500 external users.

The answer is:

A. Yes

This is calling out the Azure Graph API CMDlet New-MgInvitation, which is the equivalent of the Azure AD Cmdlet New-AzureADMSInvitation.

60)

1) Yes, You can assign users MS Defender for Cloud Apps on a per user basis.

2) No, You cannot remove the P2 license as User1 is in Group1.

3) No, nested group assignments don't work

Extra explanation:

1) Yes: The "Microsoft Defender for Cloud Apps Discovery" license is not automatically assigned through Group1 (but it's also not prohibited).

2) NO: The "Azure Active Directory Premium P2 License" is automatically assigned to the user. If I could remove the license from the user afterwards, it would contradict the "Assignment option" of Group1.

3) NO: User2 is in Group2, which is a member of Group1. However, license assignments are not inherited through subgroups (I don't have a Microsoft source for this statement).

Reference:

https://learn.microsoft.com/en-us/azure/active-directory/enterprise-users/licensing-group-advanced

End of Practice Test II

Feel free to reach out to me anytime, and don't forget to connect with me on LinkedIn: Georgio Daccache. I'm always

available to provide additional
assistance and support.

Good Luck

www.ingramcontent.com/pod-product-compliance
Lightning Source LLC
LaVergne TN
LVHW051434050326
832903LV00030BD/3082